Narratives of Political Violence

An exploration of how political violence is constructed; this book presents the life stories of individuals once committed to political transformation through violent means in Portugal.

Challenging simplistic conceptualisations about the actors of violence, this book examines issues of temporality, gender and interpersonal dynamics in the study of political violence. It is the first comprehensive case study of political violence in Portugal, based on the perspectives of former militants. These are individuals from different political spheres who became convinced that they could not be mere spectators of the circumstances of their times. For them, the only viable way of making a difference was through violent acts. Applying the Dialogical Self Theory to trace the identity positions underpinning their narratives, this book not only sheds light on radicalisation and deradicalisation processes at the individual level, but also on the meso- and macro-level contexts that instigate engagement with and encourage disengagement from armed organisations.

This book will be of interest to students and scholars of critical terrorism studies, political violence, European history and security studies more generally.

Raquel da Silva is a British Academy Postdoctoral Fellow in the International Development Department, University of Birmingham, UK.

Routledge Critical Terrorism Studies

Series Editor: Richard Jackson
University of Otago, New Zealand

This book series will publish rigorous and innovative studies on all aspects of terrorism, counter-terrorism and state terror. It seeks to advance a new generation of thinking on traditional subjects and investigate topics frequently overlooked in orthodox accounts of terrorism. Books in this series will typically adopt approaches informed by critical-normative theory, post-positivist methodologies and non-Western perspectives, as well as rigorous and reflective orthodox terrorism studies.

Hamas, Jihad and Popular Legitimacy
Reinterpreting Resistance in Palestine
Tristan Dunning

Terrorism, Talking and Transformation
A Critical Approach
Harmonie Toros

Russia's Securitization of Chechnya
How War Became Acceptable
Julie Wilhelmsen

A Critical Theory of Counterterrorism
Ontology, Epistemology and Normativity
Sondre Lindahl

Narratives of Political Violence
Life Stories of Former Militants
Raquel da Silva

For more information about this series, please visit: https://www.routledge.com/Routledge-Critical-Terrorism-Studies/book-series/RCTS

Narratives of Political Violence

Life Stories of Former Militants

Raquel da Silva

Routledge
Taylor & Francis Group
LONDON AND NEW YORK

First published 2019
by Routledge
2 Park Square, Milton Park, Abingdon, Oxon OX14 4RN

and by Routledge
711 Third Avenue, New York, NY 10017

Routledge is an imprint of the Taylor & Francis Group, an informa business

British Library Cataloguing in Publication Data
A catalogue record for this book is available from the British Library

Library of Congress Cataloging in Publication Data
A catalog record has been requested for this book

ISBN: 978-1-138-54252-5 (hbk)
ISBN: 978-1-351-00840-2 (ebk)

Typeset in Times New Roman
by Taylor & Francis Books

MIX
Paper from responsible sources
FSC www.fsc.org FSC® C013604

Printed by CPI Group (UK) Ltd, Croydon CR0 4YY

Dedication: For Carla Machado, who planted the seed of this book; and for Filipe, whose steadfast support allowed me to make it a reality.

Contents

Illustrations

Figures

Tables

Acknowledgements

This book is the result of having dedicated a good part of the last decade of my life to the study of political violence in Portugal. I want to start by thanking all the Portuguese women and men who shared their life stories with me. I thank them for their trust, empathy and respect. I am also thankful to the Foundation for Science and Technology which funded much of the research for this book.

Throughout this journey, the unwavering support of several people has been essential to keep me going, to keep me sane and to keep me joyful. I am very grateful to Nicolas Lemay-Hébert, whose role as dissertation advisor and mentor has been invaluable. He has never been too busy to care for my project, to listen to me or to help me work out what to do next. His energy and passion are contagious and I am very fortunate to have knocked on the right door!

I want to thank Richard Jackson for supporting this project from day one and for all the useful advice which led me not only to turn my doctoral dissertation into a book, but to develop my research further through this book. This was also made possible through the work I developed with the amazing team of researchers from the Change Processes in Psychotherapy Research Group at the University of Minho, Portugal, in particular Catarina Rosa, Joana Silva, Pablo Férnandez-Navarro, and Miguel M. Gonçalves. They introduced me to Dialogical Self Theory and helped me to take the first steps towards the analytical framework developed in this book. Their support has proved indispensable.

The relationship with the fantastic people at the Centre for Narrative Research at the University of East London – Molly Andrews, Cigdem Esin, Aura Lounasmaa, to name just a few – has also been a source of motivation. Their annual postgraduate research conference – "To Think is to Experiment" – provided a venue to test my ideas, gain inspiration and learn more about narrative research. The same applies to the ConnectFutures team – Zubeda Limbada, Laura Zahra McDonald, and Lynn Davis. I admire their commitment to social justice and thank them for welcoming me into the team, and for their friendship and ongoing support. I am also very grateful to Jeremy Hollow and Michael Jaxa-Chamiec from Listen and Learn Research, who over the years have been infinitely patient and kind to me. Working with them helped me grow as a researcher and as a team member. I thank them for their example and for all the fun we have had together.

I also want to thank all the people who gave me feedback on my writing at various stages: Airi Lampinen, Josefin Graef, Ruth Densham, Diana Quigley, Molly Andrews, Paul Jackson, Catarina Rosa, Miguel M. Gonçalves, Jon Catling, Monica Pinilla-Roncancio, Debs Condy, Susanna Samson, Julia Cole, Rosey Meiring, Emily Lange, Paddy Greenleaf, Sanne Weber, Megan Armstrong, Laura Zahra McDonald, Lynn Davis, Simon De Lay, Tom Hewitt, and Lou Carter. A big thank you to Alexandre Cardoso, who took the time to understand my rough sketches of figures and tables, then helped me improve them.

Parts of Chapter 3 appeared in: Da Silva, R. (2017) 'Narrative resources and political violence: the life stories of former clandestine militants in Portugal', Contemporary Social Sciences, 12(1–2), pp. 40–51, © Academy of Social Sciences, reprinted by permission of Taylor & Francis Ltd (www.tandfonline.com) on behalf of the Academy of Social Sciences. Parts of Chapter 5 appeared in: Da Silva, R., Fernández-Navarro, P., Gonçalves, M. M., Rosa, C. and Silva, J. (2018) 'Disengagement from political violence and deradicalisation: a narrative-dialogical perspective', Studies in Conflict and Terrorism, doi: 10.1080/1057610X.2018.1452709, © Academy of Social Sciences, reprinted by permission of Taylor & Francis Ltd (www.tandfonline.com) on behalf of the Academy of Social Sciences. I am grateful to Taylor and Francis for permission to use the material in this book, and to my co-authors of the second article.

Without the moral and practical support of my family and friends, writing this book would never have been possible. I am very thankful for each one of them and for everything they have done for me. I want to thank in particular Ruth and John Mountford for their acts of love and kindness towards me and my family. They are our English family and Ruth bakes the best chocolate cake ever! Ellen O'Brien has also been a great source of support and encouragement. There are no words to thank my mother and my parents-in-law for all the childcare they have done while I worked on this book and for all their love and support. Last but never least, I thank Filipe and Gabriel, who are immeasurably more than all I asked or imagined.

List of abbreviations

ARA	*Acção Revolucionária Armada* / Revolutionary Armed Action
BR	*Brigadas Revolucionárias* / Revolutionary Brigades
CTS	Critical Terrorism Studies
DST	Dialogical Self Theory
ELP	*Exército de Libertação de Portugal* / Portuguese Liberation Army
FP-25	*Forças Populares 25 de Abril* / Popular Forces of 25 April
FRELIMO	*Frente de Libertação de Moçambique* / Mozambique's Liberation Front
LUAR	*Liga de Unidade e Acção Revolucionária* / League of Unity and Revolutionary Action
MDLP	*Movimento Democrático para a Libertação de Portugal* / Democratic Movement for the Liberation of Portugal
MFA	*Movimento das Forças Armadas* / Armed Forces Movement
MPLA	*Movimento para a Libertação de Angola* / Movement for the Liberation of Angola
PAIGC	*Partido Africano para a Independência da Guiné e de Cabo Verde* / African Party for the Independence of Guinea and Cape Verde
PCP	*Partido Comunista Português* / Portuguese Communist Party
PREC	*Processo Revolucionário em Curso* / Ongoing Revolutionary Process
PRP/BR	*Partido Revolucionário do Proletariado/Brigadas Revolucionárias* / Revolutionary Party of the Proletariat/Revolutionary Brigades
PSD	*Partido Social Democrata* / Social Democratic Party
UNITA	*União Nacional para a Independência Total de Angola* / National Union for the Total Independence of Angola

Introduction

Artur: the journey to being a martyr-hero

Artur starts by telling me that his village was "very Catholic" and "very *salazarista*", which means that almost everyone supported Salazar's authoritarian regime known as the *Estado Novo* (literally "New State"). The same applied to his family:

> From my father's side, there was a priest … and there was also a nun … and one part of my family was *salazarista*, fascist, and pro-Hitler during the war. The other part was republican, secular, and social democrat. And then there was my father, who was more communist.

His father had been an immigrant in the United States of America, which seemed to have influenced his political views. According to Artur, "Whoever went to the Soviet Union would come back right-wing, reactionary, and fascist. Whoever went to the capital of entrepreneurship, to the United States, would return half communist, which happened to my father". At home, his father would talk about the Soviet Union and even had a picture of Lenin on the wall, despite nobody knowing who he was, but he never talked about the Portuguese Communist Party (PCP): "Probably he feared that I would associate myself with the Communist Party and then something could happen to me". However, his father's fears became reality when in 1959 Artur joined the PCP, and in 1964 he went underground to found the party's armed arm, the ARA (Acção Revolucionária Armada / Revolutionary Armed Action).

Artur's decision was motivated by his views on the contextual circumstances of his time, the existence of an oppressive regime – the *Estado Novo* – that had been in power for almost forty years, not allowing any form of alternative political choice and violently repressing any dissidents. However, even with such a context in mind, Artur considered that going underground was "a very violent thing" – an expression that describes a very difficult experience, both emotionally and physically. Making such a choice completely disrupts one's life:

> [I]t was a very difficult decision in my life, because I knew what I was getting involved in, and what I was leaving behind – my family, all my friends, not friendship in itself, but relationships with people, leaving my degree unfinished … [W]ell, it would be a radical change in my life.

Nevertheless, Artur believes that his choice was justified because of the position he occupied in that particular moment in time and space, in that particular context which framed the decision to commit his life to a clandestine, politically violent organisation. This was a position that made him choose "martyrdom" of his self-interests for a greater good:

> In all wars, there is always one of those heroes, a martyr-hero, who instantly throws himself onto the grenade that is about to blow up to save the fifteen or twenty comrades fighting around him. So, these things are highly dependent on context, aren't they?

Afonso: defending against communism

Afonso believes the political education he received at home prevented him from embarking on the "ideological drifts" that happened to some young people after the revolution of 25 April 1974. Such a revolution brought the *Estado Novo* regime to an end and put in place a process towards the establishment of democracy. At his home, during mealtimes, the family did not discuss money or other people, but there were plenty of topics of conversation: "International politics was one of the themes that my father used to develop. My mother talked more about religion. She was a great activist in social work".

Afonso also believes that his military training and participation in the Colonial War were push factors in the context of his involvement with the ELP (Exército de Libertação de Portugal / Portuguese Liberation Army) after the revolution. For him, the Colonial War was about "defence missions" liberating both the settlers and the natives from the extreme violence of the communist guerrilla movements, which were undermining the great work done by the Portuguese regime in the development of the colonies. From his position as a military man, defending his nation, Afonso could not accept the decolonisation process that took place after the revolution. What is more, on his return to Portugal, he found that "things that had nothing to do with democracy" were taking place, which put the country "in a situation of open violence". He thought "the situation was getting out of hand" because the PCP was clearly already commanding operations in Portugal. However, the problem was that "the Portuguese people, who were not communist, were afraid". Therefore, he felt it necessary "to prove that the PCP was a minority, that the PCP could be made afraid, if necessary, and that the majority of the Portuguese people was not communist".

Afonso acknowledges that the ELP aimed to drag the populace into revolt and target PCP's headquarters, in order to prove that "the Portuguese people were not communist" and did not want communism installed in Portugal.

However, at the same time, he emphasises that the ELP followed Christian principles, so gratuitous violence was not an option. Thus, he feels that his organisation was faithful to higher principles and defended a righteous cause, leaving him with a clear conscience and a belief that he fulfilled his obligations: "I am glad to have been able to do what I did, both in the military and afterwards. I even take a certain pride in it".

Mariana: a natural disposition to a violent response

When asked what made her "available" to the armed struggle, Mariana answers that she had been available since she was born. She was "born and bred in fascism", which, in her opinion, accounted for a "very reactionary training". At the origin of her political awareness she places her mother's tales of a republican grandfather who was "systematically arrested". Mariana's mother's intention was to discourage her children's involvement in politics, but the stories only increased their curiosity and enthusiasm. Then came the death of her father, which caused the family to become intimately acquainted with financial hardship, and, finally, her involvement with the very active and oppositional student movement: "I was having political meetings at age fourteen, listening to Zeca Afonso[1] and reading Trotsky's books in secret".

All of this helped to convince Mariana that she possessed "a natural predisposition to respond" to social injustice. Unlike her friends at school, she "used to think about stuff" and used her "head for something else besides growing hair". Social injustice, such as that perpetrated during the Colonial War, bothered her, as did incidents at home, especially the political police's assassination of the law student Ribeiro dos Santos in 1972. This event precipitated Mariana's first arrest at the age of fourteen because she was caught sticking up a poster of Dos Santos. She was also very politically active at school, where she was involved in "all school wars", and made preparations for the revolution that she believed was inevitable: "At secondary school, I was always part of student organisations. When 25 April came, I was waiting for it. There were rumours. I was sixteen and I knew; I was organised. So, when 25 April happened, I was more than available!"

This availability took the form of Mariana's involvement with a couple of radical left-wing (but legal) political parties from the age of sixteen, and her subsequent recruitment to an armed organisation at the age of nineteen, which made her very proud. She always believed that violence was essential for social and political change and that pacifism was disappointing. Thus, she supported ETA, the IRA, and the Red Brigades until she had an opportunity to participate in the struggle herself. In this vein, she proudly affirms:

> I did not stay at home waiting for something to fall from the sky. I went to war, I took part in the struggle. I fought, I was there, I did not stay put. I did it all, me and my partner. We gave everything we could give.

Outline of this study

These and other life stories of former politically violent militants in Portugal are the topic of this book. Individual radical dispositions are often deemed as the primary drivers of political violence. However, when such dispositions are disconnected from biographical experiences and contextual factors, the result may be flat and limited descriptions and explanations that lack the complexity and richness of intertwined individual, social, cultural, political, and historical processes. Thus, the theorisation of the life stories of former politically violent militants is a new and welcome development in the political violence literature. As such, this book is about much more than specific life stories. It represents a case study that contributes to our understanding of politically motivated violence within different socio-political contexts, extending the findings of earlier studies that have incorporated the perspectives of the politically violent militants (see, e.g., Horgan, 2009; Toros, 2012; della Porta, 2013; Heath-Kelly, 2013).

Why do individuals engage in violent militancy? How are they radicalised? Why do men and women commit their lives to politically violent organisations? Why do they ultimately leave violence behind? Can they be deradicalised? The answers to these questions are not linear, but life story scholars consider that individuals respond to the conditions and stimuli of their environment in ways that are consistent with the storylines of their lives. In other words, they behave in ways that are consistent with the perceptions they hold about themselves, others and their political, social, cultural, economic, and historical milieu (see, e.g., McAdams, 2008). Such perceptions are generated by a personal cultural repertoire, which is influenced by the "early narrative environment of the family", by the stories individuals access while growing up (Wang and Brockmeier, 2002, p. 54), and by the social interactions that occur across their life course (Elder, 1994). Thus, individuals' perceptions differ significantly according to the cultural resources that are available to them (Ochs and Capps, 1996; Brockmeier, 2009).

Through the stories of Artur, Afonso, and Mariana, it is possible to see how historical moments and places shaped their political awareness, influencing their engagement with an armed organisation. Both Artur and Afonso reached their youth during the *Estado Novo* regime. However, while Artur was brought up in an environment that offered him some anti-regime notions, Afonso was raised by supporters of Salazar. Artur went to university, which was an environment populated by oppositional political narratives. Afonso chose a military career and went on to defend the Portuguese colonies in Africa. Later, Artur (whom I consider a pre-revolution militant) founded an armed organisation to overthrow the regime and end the Colonial War, while Afonso (whom I consider a counter-revolution militant) founded an armed organisation to stop a potential communist takeover of Portugal following the April Revolution. Thus, although they belonged to the same generation, pre- and counter-revolution militants chose to "work up the material of their common experiences in different and specific ways" (Mannheim, 1952,

p. 304). Finally, Mariana (whom I consider a post-revolution militant) built her narrative identity through seeing herself as a “product” of the April Revolution – which took place when she was very young – and all of the intense political activity and political narratives that surrounded it. She was strongly influenced by the cultural meanings of her environment, which in turn influenced the course of her life story (Brockmeier, 2009) and crafted the episodic particulars of her autobiographical memory, shaping her narrative identity (McAdams and McLean, 2013). Throughout their adolescence and youth, Artur, Afonso, and Mariana used their contextual variables as building blocks to form their life stories, moulding their personal narratives according to the moment in history when they were living (Habermas and Hatiboğlu, 2014).

This book is motivated by two goals. First, I intend to give centre stage to the life stories of individuals who were once committed to political transformation via violent means in Portugal. These individuals were convinced that they could not be mere spectators of the political circumstances of their times. For them, the only viable way to make a difference was through violent acts. Therefore, I provide a platform for individuals whose voices are typically not heard or taken into account, and whose lives represent narratives that are usually excluded from official histories. Irrespective of the reasons for such exclusion, be they related to stronger ideological tales taking precedence or to the teller’s character being considered dubious, politically motivated violence perpetrated by non-state actors did take place in Portugal and it did not appear out of thin air.

My second goal in writing this book is to provide a dialogical narrative identity analytical framework to make sense of the life stories of former politically violent militants. Such a framework is composed of three distinctive drivers of individual agency in the context of political violence: engagement with, life within, and disengagement from a politically violent organisation. This framework is underpinned by the analysis of life stories of former militants in light of Dialogical Self Theory (DST). This may be applied to different cases in order to analyse and understand politically violent militancy in the context of the broader life stories of its actors, as well as the political narratives surrounding them. I believe that by focusing on the journeys of involvement with, life within, and disengagement from a politically violent organisation (i.e., micro-level context) it is possible to shed light on radicalisation and deradicalisation processes at the individual level, but also on the macro- and meso-level contexts that instigate engagement with and encourage disengagement from armed organisations.

In order to achieve these goals, this book takes on board the perspectives of twenty-eight former politically violent militants who belonged to a total of six different armed organisations. Four of these organisations leaned towards the left of the political spectrum and two to the right. Three were active prior to the revolution of 25 April 1974, in dictatorial conditions. The other three were active after the revolution, in democratic conditions. The variety of organisations and people under study reveals that this is a complex topic; hence, this book reflects a diversity of experiences and understandings and explores the socio-political specificities of a country at a time when it was the scene of violent conflict.

In this vein, by exploring how politically motivated violence came to form part of several individuals' life courses, I examine the contexts that surrounded their militancy (e.g., historical – forty years of an oppressive regime; social – growing up listening to tales of family resistance); what their past militancy, and in some cases present activism, means for them (e.g., martyrdom of personal interests in order to achieve a greater good); how it impacted on their lives in different moments (e.g., while living underground, after release from prison); and how a few women, against all societal expectations, including in some cases the expectations of their own male comrades, played active roles within armed organisations, dealt with gender-motivated conflict, and became symbols of emancipation.

Who should read this book?

In the remaining chapters, I act as a "story analyst": that is, I adopt an interpretive rather than a purely descriptive approach, using my own theoretical and analytical lens to make sense of individual accounts. As a result, I have produced a "realist tale" which allows "spaces for participant voices to be heard in a coherent text, and with specific points in mind … [to] provide compelling, detailed, and complex depictions of a social world" (Sparkes, 2002, p. 55). In this sense, my voice as a researcher in the interpretive process is interactive. I examine the intricate interactions between former politically violent militants and myself.

It is also important to underline that perceiving the self as always multiple and multivocal, and working from an interpretive rather than a purely descriptive approach does not allow me to give a voice to – or speak for – the people I met. Rather, when I argue that I am giving them a voice, I mean that I am speaking about the words I have obtained from them. I am representing some of their selves which were co-constructed through dialogue, interpersonal interactions, and perceptions regarding who I am and the audience I represent. Thus, in order to be transported into the frameworks of meaning of other people, whose life circumstances are very different from my own, I resort to what Martha Nussbaum has called "the narrative imagination":

> This means the ability to think what it might be like to be in the shoes of a person different from oneself, to be an intelligent reader of that person's story, and to understand the emotions and wishes and desires that someone so placed might have.
>
> (Nussbaum, 1997, pp. 10–11)

How is this relevant for our theoretical and methodological understandings of political violence? For *researchers of political violence*, I offer the theorisation of the life stories of former politically violent militants. I add descriptive depth and conceptual sophistication to existent understandings of political violence. I also demonstrate how the life stories of former militants seem to be strongly connected to the political narratives that inhabit their spatial and temporal coordinates. This offers a new way of thinking about individuals who chose to commit part of their lives to political transformation via violent means, but who are not simply violent militants. These are individuals who have had previous personal, social, and political experiences that made them available to such a choice; but they have also had other aspirations that were not related to politically motivated violence (e.g., careers, families). In addition, tracing the repertoire of identity positions throughout the three phases in the journeys of former militants – engagement with, life within, and disengagement from a politically violent organisation – advances the research in this area in three distinct analytical aspects: the decisional contexts involved in different moments of time in the life of a politically violent militant; the choices made by individuals who have been part of a politically violent organisation; and the nature and implications for individuals of different types of politically violent organisations, whose existence and structure were closely connected to the socio-political context of their time. I consider that such a framework to study political violence allows an understanding of the diversity that characterises politically violent militants, whose pathways into, within, and out of armed organisations vary across spatial and temporal contexts. In this sense, analysing political violence in context connects it to the structural violence in which it frequently occurs, generating multiple identities for the politically violent militants and rejecting the label "terrorist" as biased, judgemental, and of little explanatory value.

For *practitioners dealing with political violence*, one of the strengths of the framework developed in this book is its potential application to support both prevention and intervention work. In relation to prevention work, I do not mean singling out particular individuals who are perceived as being at risk of engagement with an armed organisation, or criminalising the pre-criminal space. I am talking about prevention programmes that build resilience against violence and extremism. These may take place in schools, community centres, religious institutions, and even prisons. Understanding the life stories and experiences of former militants enables practitioners, such as teachers and youth workers, to develop adequate counter-narratives and to facilitate the construction of more resilient selves. My analytical framework can equally assist intervention work with individuals who have been convicted of terrorism offences, including returnees who have participated in conflicts overseas. By promoting an understanding of the complex range of factors behind engagement and radicalisation, as well as disengagement and deradicalisation, such a framework rejects a one-size-fits-all model. On the contrary, it allows for recognition of both micro-level (e.g., personal aims, loyalties, priorities, grievances) and macro-level drivers (e.g., collective narratives, cultural resources), and the reasons for their change or maintenance over time.

Understanding these aspects allows practitioners, such as social workers and psychologists, to identify the areas that need to be worked on and to look for alternative ways that will allow individuals to pursue their aims through legal means.

For *researchers of political narratives*, the methodological contribution of my research is linked to the work done by Critical Terrorism Studies (CTS) scholars since the early 2000s. These scholars have highlighted the need to establish narrative as an approach to study political violence and have worked on the notion of temporality in this arena (Jackson, Jarvis, Gunning and Smyth, 2011; Heath-Kelly, Jarvis and Baker-Beall, 2014). However, while these scholars have been mainly focused on the narratives of the "war on terror" and counter-terrorism narratives, very little critical research has looked specifically at the life stories of former politically violent militants. Thus, my empirical application of a dialogical narrative identity approach, informed by DST, has critical implications for the field of political narratives as a method of social inquiry. For instance, this methodological approach shows that the stories individuals tell about their past experiences are influenced by how they construct their present selves, the narratives they intend to corroborate or oppose, and who is listening. Stories are not only narratively performed and impacted by others; they are also actors in people's lives, triggering decisions and behaviours (Frank, 2010). Consequently, this study contributes to our understanding of the performative abilities of stories in people's lives and the role of the complex and dynamic identity system of each individual.

For *historians of Portugal*, this book offers a novel perspective on the contexts that gave rise to armed struggle, how that struggle was fought, and its consequences. This perspective is built on the tales of political violence offered by men and women who participated in it. In this book, I quote their voices extensively in order to bring to life their experiences, thoughts, and emotions, but also to counter the tendency to silence their stories, which has been the norm in the Portuguese "battle over memory", as coined by Manuel Loff (2014, p. 10). According to this author, this tendency took root because their activities were linked to events such as the April Revolution, which themselves have been politically and socially depreciated in mainstream political narratives. This is something that the Portuguese historian Rui Bebiano calls "unmemory", rather than "forgetfulness", because while the latter involves "carelessness, accident, casual blur of past reminiscences", the former involves "a voluntary erasure of memory, a lack of knowledge or even a lack of interest in certain areas of living, considered irrelevant and not instrumental" (Bebiano, 2006, p. 9).

Finally, *the general reader* will find that this book provides an opportunity to come into contact with and reflect upon the life stories of former politically violent militants. My analysis presents each individual as a whole person, as a human being whose actions are not only violent, and have not always been nor always will be. In this book, all readers will meet political actors who are "fellow human beings and not dog-headed cannibals" (Leach, 1977, p. 36), people whose lives are influenced and influence their spatial, temporal, and relational contexts and are liable to change.

Outline of subsequent chapters

In Chapter 1, I provide a brief historical contextualisation of the emergence of the various non-state politically violent organisations under analysis and the main characteristics of each. I assume that many English-speaking readers may not be familiar with contemporary Portuguese history, so I believe it is helpful to provide some background information regarding the *Estado Novo* regime, the revolution of 25 April 1974, and the counter-revolution of 25 November 1975.

In Chapter 2, I detail the conceptual framework behind this book. I argue that the application of the core commitments of CTS in conjunction with a narrative approach can contribute to the theorisation of the life stories of former politically violent militants and provide rich descriptions of political violence. I also establish my DST-informed dialogical narrative identity analytical framework to trace the identity positions underpinning former militants' political narratives of engagement with, life within, and disengagement from politically violent organisations. Finally, I elaborate on my approach to data co-creation and analysis.

Chapters 3, 4, and 5 constitute the empirical chapters, which address the processes of engagement with, life within, and disengagement from politically violent organisations. As noted by Catarina Rosa and Miguel Gonçalves (2008), the ability of infinitely reformulating the identity positions' repertoire can be seen as a play in several acts. In this sense, each of these chapters corresponds to an act, where personal, social, political, and historical circumstances influence which identity positions take the leading role, while other voices are relegated to the background. Thus, in Chapter 3, I explore the origins of personal political awareness, which are closely linked to different socialisation agents, such as family members, and I tackle the dynamics of commitment to an armed organisation, which in many cases resulted in a total break in the militants' life courses.

Chapter 4 explores individual experiences lived within politically violent organisations. In this chapter, I discuss the dynamics of life under a clandestine identity, including the process of going underground, the challenges of the underground life, and the gender dynamics among clandestine militants. I also address the use of violence for political means, particularly in relation to the perspectives, personal experiences, and emotions that surrounded the commission of politically violent acts.

Chapter 5 focuses on the influencing factors, reasons, incentives, and barriers presented by those engaged in political violence when ending their commitment to an organisation. I also explore how former militants rework their pasts in the present, reflecting on their memories, on the moments and events that marked their lives, and on who they became.

In the Conclusion, I return to the question of how the storylines, in which former politically violent militants in Portugal were moulded as subjects through their interactions with the social and political contexts of their time, influenced their involvement with armed organisations and how they act at the service of their present selves. I conclude that a narrative-based framework of analysis, which takes into consideration individuals' life stories, not only informs our understandings of the Portuguese armed struggle but also holds the potential for extending our knowledge of engagement and disengagement, radicalisation and deradicalisation processes across a number of other contexts of politically violent militancy.

Note

1 Zeca Afonso's music played a significant role in the resistance movement against the *Estado Novo* regime.

References

Bebiano, R. (2006) 'Da desmemória e do seu antídoto', in Cruzeiro, M. and Bebiano, R. (eds) *Anos inquietos: vozes do movimento estudantil em Coimbra (1961–1974)*. Porto: Edições Afrontamento, pp. 9–14.

Brockmeier, J. (2009) 'Reaching for meaning: human agency and the narrative imagination', *Theory and Psychology*, 19(2), pp. 213–233.

della Porta, D. (2013) *Clandestine political violence*. Cambridge: Cambridge University Press.

Elder, G. (1994) 'Time, human agency and social change: perspectives on the life course', *Social Psychology Quarterly*, 57(1), pp. 4–15.

Frank, A. (2010) *Letting stories breathe*. Chicago: University of Chicago Press.

Habermas, T. and Hatiboğlu, N. (2014) 'Contextualizing the self: the emergence of a biographical understanding in adolescence', *New Directions for Child and Adolescent Development*, 145, pp. 29–41.

Heath-Kelly, C. (2013) *Politics of violence: militancy, international politics, killing in the name*. London: Routledge.

Heath-Kelly, C., Jarvis, L. and Baker-Beall, C. (2014) 'Editors' introduction: Critical Terrorism Studies: practice, limits and experience', *Critical Studies on Terrorism*, 7 (1), pp. 1–10.

Horgan, J. (2009) 'Individual disengagement: a psychological analysis', in Bjørgo, T. and Horgan, J. (eds) *Leaving terrorism behind: individual and collective disengagement*. New York: Routledge, pp. 17–29.

Horgan, J. and Taylor, M. (2011) 'Disengagement, de-radicalization and the arc of terrorism: future directions for research', in Coolsaet, R. (ed.) *Jihadi terrorism and the radicalisation challenge: European and American experiences*. 2nd Edition. Surrey: Ashgate, pp. 173–186.

Jackson, R., Jarvis, L., Gunning, J. and Smyth, M. (2011) *Terrorism: a critical introduction*. Basingstoke: Palgrave Macmillan.

Leach, E. (1977) *Custom, law and terroristic violence*. Edinburgh: Edinburgh University Press.

Loff, M. (2014) 'Dictatorship and revolution: socio-political reconstructions of collective memory in post-authoritarian Portugal', *Culture and History Digital Journal*, 3 (2), pp. 1–13.

Mannheim, K. (1952) 'The problem of generations', in Kecskemet, P. (ed.) *Essays on the sociology of knowledge.* London: Routledge & Kegan Paul.

McAdams, D. (2008) 'Personal narratives and the life story: theory and research', in John, O., Robins, R. and Pervin, L. (eds) *Handbook of personality: theory and research.* 3rd Edition. New York: Guilford Press, pp. 241–261.

McAdams, D. P. and McLean, K. C. (2013) 'Narrative identity', *Current Directions in Psychological Science*, 22(3), pp. 233–238.

Nussbaum, M. (1997) *Cultivating humanity.* Cambridge, MA: Harvard University Press.

Ochs, E. and Capps, L. (1996) 'Narrating the self', *Annual Review of Anthropology*, 25 (1), pp. 19–43.

Rosa, C. and Gonçalves, M. M. (2008) 'Dialogical self and close relationships: looking for ambivalences', *Studia Psychologica*, 6(8), pp. 87–106.

Sparkes, A. C. (2002) *Telling tales in sport and physical activity: a qualitative journey.* Champaign, IL: Human Kinetics Press.

Taylor, M. and Horgan, J. (2006) 'A conceptual framework for addressing psychological process in the development of the terrorist', *Terrorism and Political Violence*, 18(4), pp. 585–601.

Toros, H. (2012) *Terrorism, talking and transformation: a critical approach*. Abingdon: Routledge.

Wang, Q. and Brockmeier, J. (2002) 'Autobiographical remembering as cultural practice: understanding the interplay between memory, self and culture', *Culture and Psychology*, 8(1), pp. 45–64.

1 Political violence in context

The Portuguese armed struggle

The exercise of context reconstruction and exploration is very important for the understanding of how and why politically violent organisations came into existence in Portugal in different periods of time and in different socio-political conditions. This volume focuses solely on political violence committed by non-state actors. However, in this chapter and throughout Chapters 3, 4, and 5, the accounts provided by relevant literature and my interviewees will also touch on the issue of state violence, particularly in the *Estado Novo* period (1926–1974). This era is also known as *Salazarismo*, after its instigator and then ruler (1932–1968), António de Oliveira Salazar. *Salazarismo* represented the embodiment of power and a strong state organised around a strong individual, which it was thought could eradicate the perceived chaos of the First Republic. Salazar was the answer to the demands for an authoritarian solution from certain sectors of Portuguese society who were strongly inspired by other European examples, particularly Italy's Mussolini and Spain's Primo de Rivera. Among those sectors were reactionary factions of the bourgeoisie, a significant proportion of the Catholic Church, and some intellectuals of the First Republic. In this context, Salazar started his journey to leadership by achieving financial balance to the country as minister of finance. In 1932, he agreed to lead the government. Finally, in 1933, he presented a new constitution that gave birth to the *Estado Novo* (a designation that Salazar himself coined for the regime he intended to rule). At that time, many Portuguese viewed Salazar as the "saviour of the homeland" (Amaro, 1982, p. 1007), which was submerged in financial, political, social, and cultural turmoil – issues that he pledged to resolve.

In this chapter, I shall identify the historical and political contexts in which six politically violent organisations emerged in Portugal over the course of a quarter of a century (1962–1987). During the first wave (1962–1974), in a very clear and direct way, the *Estado Novo* regime led to the emergence of the LUAR (*Liga de Unidade e Acção Revolucionária* / League of Unity and Revolutionary Action), the ARA (*Acção Revolucionária Armada* / Revolutionary Armed Action), and the BR (*Brigadas Revolucionárias* / Revolutionary Brigades). These three organisations fought against the regime and its policies, predominantly those relating to its authoritarian, imperial, and colonial stances. They resorted to violence against a regime that in their eyes was extremely violent and repressive and could not be defeated by peaceful means. The latter had been tried for years without success and at a high personal cost for numerous individuals who suffered arrest, torture, and forced labour.

In the second wave (1975–1976), the rise of the ELP (*Exército de Libertação de Portugal* / Portuguese Liberation Army) and the MDLP (*Movimento Democrático para a Libertação de Portugal* / Democratic Movement for the Liberation of Portugal) was triggered by fears of a possible communist takeover following the April Revolution and by antipathy towards some of the decisions taken by the provisional government (e.g., the decolonisation process). These organisations essentially comprised right-wing military personnel, who usually leaned towards the deposed regime.

In the third wave (1980–1987), the creation of the FP-25 (*Forças Populares 25 de Abril* / Popular Forces of 25 April) was motivated by a belief that the principles espoused by the April Revolution were starting to fade away, which was facilitating the re-emergence of the unjust society of the Salazar years. For some individuals, this situation could be resolved by nothing less than a socialist revolution.

Figure 1.1 provides a timeline of both the main historical events that set the context for the rise of armed organisations in Portugal and the periods when these organisations were active.

In the beginning was Salazar

The *Estado Novo* is a period of Portuguese history that has its origins in the military coup of 28 May 1926. This coup ended the First Republic, which had only begun on 5 October 1910 after ninety years of constitutional monarchy (1820–1910). The First Republic was always plagued by great difficulties of consolidation, as Fernando Rosas (1989a) explains. For instance, in the course of its sixteen years, there were forty-five governments and ten coup attempts. Moreover, in 1918, one of the First Republic's eight presidents, Sidónio Pais, was assassinated. Thus, while the military dictatorship established after the coup of 28 May 1926 did not have a well-defined ideology, it was deeply sceptical about the effectiveness of parliamentary democracy and it aimed to restore the Catholic Church's paramount role in the socio-political life of the country (Baiôa, 1994).

In the first months of the military dictatorship, the fight for power between liberal–republican and conservative factions was won by the latter. However, there were two different groups of conservatives: one that advocated conservative republicanism and another that supported Salazar (Pinto and Rezola, 2007). The first group considered the military dictatorship as a necessary but transitory regime whose role would end once order was restored and a constitutional regime secured. However, it had a poorly defined strategy of government, weak internal cohesion and weak leadership, all of which contributed to its ultimate

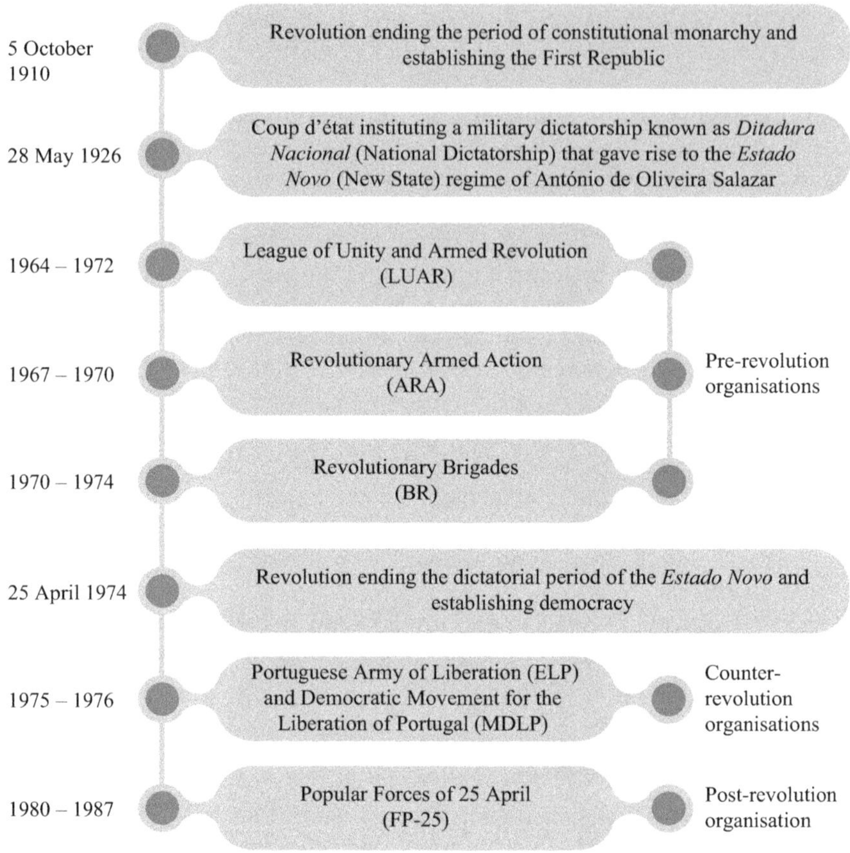

Figure 1.1 Timeline

failure. A financial and economic crisis ensued, which meant that all attention and hope for the future turned to Salazar. This figure from the Catholic centre had extensively criticised the financial policies implemented by the conservatives who headed the first government, having resigned from his role as economist in the cabinet due to the continuing social and political instability. Nevertheless, in 1928, Salazar accepted an invitation to head the Ministry of Finance, which made him a very powerful minister in the difficult financial situation that Portugal was experiencing (Wheeler and Opello, 2010). In addition to his financial solution for the country, which envisaged a balanced economy and kept him in the same position through several changes of government, he developed a political programme – the foundation of a new political, economic and social order based on an authoritarian state (Oliveira, 1990). Thus, Salazar's political plans developed in his first years in office, culminating in the promulgation of a new constitution, as represented in Figure 1.2.

In order to accomplish his mission, Salazar based his regime on a mythical idea of nationhood. Also, similarly to Europe's fascist regimes, he aimed to

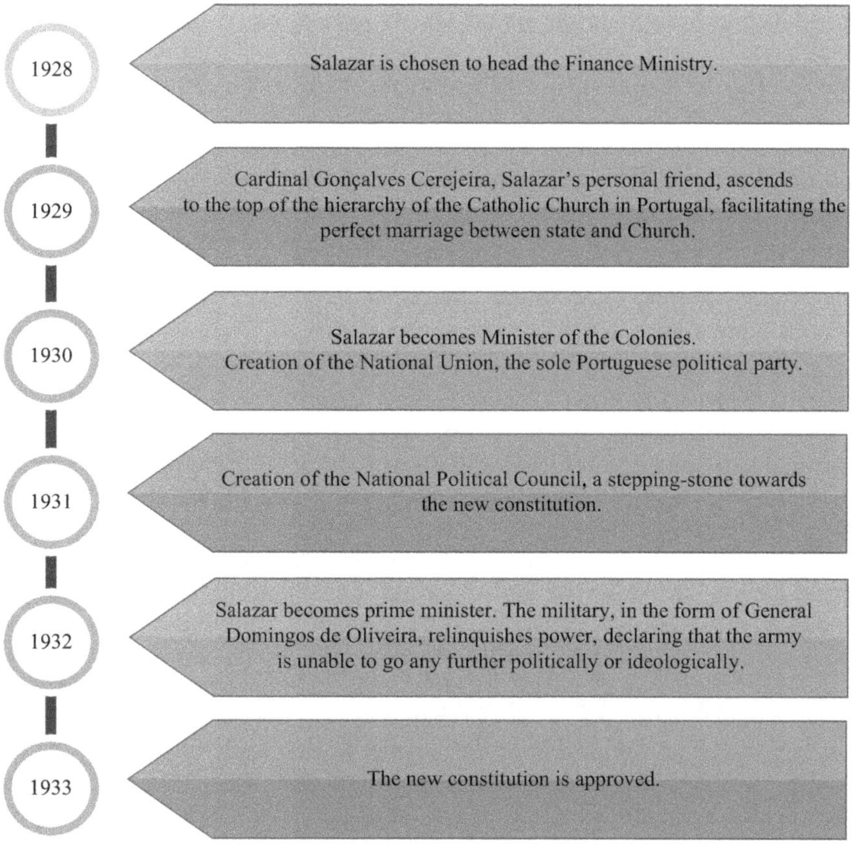

Figure 1.2 Salazar's consolidation in office

create a new type of Portuguese citizen, regenerated by the regime's ideology. Such an ideological totalising project had its apogee in the 1930s and 1940s and defined an aggressive propaganda discourse that aimed to re-educate the Portuguese people in the context of a regenerated nation (Rosas, 2001). These stances embodied by the *Estado Novo* were summarised by Salazar himself in a speech he delivered in 1936 to mark the tenth anniversary of the military coup. This speech clearly infantilised the Portuguese people and neutralised their freedom of thought, speech, organisation, and emancipation:

> To the souls torn by doubt and negativity of the present century, we look to restore the comfort of the great certainties. We do not discuss God and Virtue. We do not discuss the Nation and its History. We do not discuss Authority and its Prestige. We do not discuss Family and its Morals. We do not discuss the glory of work and duty.
>
> (Salazar, 1946, p. 130)

In order to exercise its authority as widely as possible, the *Estado Novo* fashioned and implemented a number of societal structures. Among those, three were central to triggering the activities of armed organisations in Portugal. First, there was the absence of political freedom. The multi-party system was deemed disruptive to the unity of the nation because different parties were viewed as representing individual ideas and interests. Therefore, only one party was allowed: the *União Nacional* (National Union). Moreover, the 1933 constitution granted vast powers to the president of the Council, including the ability to legislate by decree, to appoint and remove members of the government, and to ratify any acts introduced by the president of the Republic (Pinto, 1999). It also mirrored the *Estado Novo*'s corporatism, which brought the socio-professional life of each individual under the auspices of the government (Lucena, 1979).

Second, there was the absence of freedom of expression. In order to control and restrict public opinion and any debate about or criticism of the regime, the *Estado Novo* implemented mass media censorship both in Portugal and abroad (Cabrera, 2014). From books to magazines, radio broadcasts to cinema, theatre shows to song lyrics, anything that could be seen as endangering the regime's interests had to go through the Censorship Bureau. This bureau created specific "criteria" to justify its "prohibition and seizure" (Fonseca, 2005, p. 22) of unacceptable material. For example, there was a long list of forbidden themes, including: political contestation, political prisoners, colonies and civil war, agrarian reform, religion, socialist ideology, poverty, peasants' and workers' living conditions, social inequality, morals, customs, and sexuality. A "rule of silence" was imposed through censorship that affected not only the mass media but also everyday life. This gave rise to "self-censorship" and "inner repression", both of which fed people's "fear of imprisonment, fear of aggression, fear of losing a job, fear of causing harm to the family, fear of being frequently bothered by anonymous phone calls, [and] finally, fear of persecution" (Gama, 2008, p. 225).

Third, there was the political police. According to Irene Pimentel (2011), this force was organised around three main functions: to dissuade the general population from conspiring against the regime; to punish individuals who tried to conspire against the regime; and to arrest individuals who were involved with subversive parties and organisations, particularly the Portuguese Communist Party (PCP). The pattern of action followed by the political police involved detention, isolation of the detainee from any contact with family members or lawyers, and physical and psychological torture. The aim was to obtain confessions of oppositional activities and to spread fear across society through the destruction of the lives of particular individuals, who would then serve as examples for others (see more in Albuquerque, 1987; Pimentel, 2007; Cardina, 2010). When asked about this institutionalised violence and the mistreatment of prisoners in 1932, Salazar suggested that such actions were justified by the nature of the prisoners ("terrible bombers") and by the need to protect vulnerable citizens ("children and helpless people"):

> I wish to inform you that it has been concluded that the mistreated detainees were always, or almost always, terrible bombers who refused to confess, despite all the skills of the police, where they had hidden their criminal and deadly weapons. Only after employing such violent means are they able to tell the truth. And I ask myself, continuing to repress such abuses, if the lives of some children and helpless people are not well worth it and do not widely justify half a dozen shoves, at the right time, to these sinister creatures.
>
> (Salazar quoted in Ferro, 1982, p. 54)

The political police also made full use of the *Colónia Penal do Tarrafal* (Tarrafal Penal Colony) in Cape Verde, commonly known as Tarrafal. Created in 1936 and falling under the authority of the political police, this was intended for "political and social detainees" (Barreto, 2000, p. 486). Often compared to Nazi concentration camps, it was a place where detained individuals were sent with no idea about the date of their trial, if they would ever receive a trial or even if they would survive, since almost 10 per cent of the prisoners died between 1936 and 1954 (32 out of 333). Detainees were not summarily executed, but in practice they could be sentenced to death in more subtle ways. There was no sanitation and very poor hygiene. Prisoners were subjected to forced labour, suffered from malnutrition, and were refused medicines and medical assistance. Punishments for misbehaviour included beatings, deliberate exposure to malaria-carrying mosquitoes by removal of mosquito nets, and incarceration in the *frigideira* (literally "frying pan"). The latter instrument of torture was a small concrete building – five to six metres long by three metres wide – built in an isolated area with no protection from the sun, no windows, and only two iron doors, one for each of its two rooms. Up to twelve detainees might be kept in one of the rooms for as long as two weeks at a time (see Oliveira, 1987). Thus, Tarrafal is considered the "quintessence of state terrorism under Salazar" – the place where a country that forbade the death penalty sent people to die (Barreto, 2000, p. 487).

The *Estado Novo* also created indoctrination organisations such as the Secretariat of National Propaganda, the Portuguese Legion, the Portuguese Youth, and the National Federation for Joy at Work (see Alves, 1997; Rosas, 2001). These organisations were used as instruments of advertising and to defend the regime by framing each person in a particular structure and enabling control of the population (Cabrera, 2014). However, the most decisive contributors to the regime's durability were its effective censorship and the activities of the political police in the fields of repression and intimidation, as well as the cohesion of the army in moments of crisis.

Finally, it is important to highlight that in popular discourse (and in the words of some of the individuals interviewed for this study), the *Estado Novo* is often termed "fascist". However, this label does not always receive full support in academic circles because, although the *Estado Novo* was certainly an authoritarian regime, it did not display all of the characteristics of a typical fascist state. For instance, the fascist dynamic where a single party mobilises the masses and seizes power was not mirrored at the commencement of the *Estado Novo*. Rather, in Portugal, a single individual took control of the government and transformed a military dictatorship into a dictatorial regime (Nolte, 1966; Pinto, 2012). Nevertheless, several scholars have countered this argument (see, e.g., Lucena, 1979; Kayman, 1987; Collotti, 1989; Rosas, 1989b, 2001) by insisting that restrictions on freedom of expression, repression of all political opposition, violence against civilians perpetrated by the political police, corporatism that eradicated the labour movement's autonomy, and state-sponsored moralising with the aim of controlling every citizen are sufficient to justify a classification of "fascism". Thus, according to Manuel de Lucena (1979, p. 48), the *Estado Novo* was "a form of fascism without a fascist movement".

Salazar ruled Portugal for thirty-five years, until 1968, when he was replaced by Marcelo Caetano due to health issues. Caetano kept the *Estado Novo* going for six more years by adopting a philosophy of managed change, which became known as *Marcelismo* (for more on this, see Rosas and Oliveira, 2004; Ramos, Sousa and Monteiro, 2009). Thus, the start of this period was labelled the *Primavera Marcelista* (Marcelist Spring) due to a number of small changes and reforms that the new prime minister implemented (e.g., a degree of economic liberalisation). This led some people to believe that the dictatorial situation in Portugal was shifting, and that political violence against the dictatorship might hamper this process. However, such hopes were quickly dashed by a wave of brutal repression enacted by the political police in the service of Caetano's regime.

Opposition to the *Estado Novo*

The implementation of Salazar's political vision generated strong opposition throughout 1931, including revolts in Madeira, the Azores, and Guinea, student demonstrations against the dictatorship in Lisbon and Oporto, and even protests by liberal conservatives who still believed in constitutional normalisation through elections (Pimentel, 2014). However, the Portuguese opposition during the *Estado Novo* was always riddled with difficulties, especially in the 1930s. As the regime consolidated its grip on power and it strengthened and organised its repression of dissenting voices, the opposition dispersed, and fascism spread throughout Europe (Raby, 1988). However, during the Second World War and its aftermath, the increasing international challenge to authoritarian regimes had consequences for the opposition in Portugal. In 1941, the PCP was able to set up a clandestine structure and begin a strategy of infiltration in the official trade unions. Across the rest of the decade and into the 1950s, various opposition movements emerged in Portugal, such as the Anti-Fascist National Unity Movement (MUNAF) and the Democratic Unity Movement (MUD). However, these organisations' activities were effectively repressed by the regime. Nevertheless, at the beginning of the 1960s, groups of individuals exiled in South America (particularly in Venezuela and Brazil) instigated some very significant actions against the *Estado Novo*. Among these were the assault on the Portuguese ocean liner *Santa Maria* in 1961, the assault on the military quarter of Beja in 1962, and, in the same year, the diversion of a TAP flight between Casablanca and Lisbon, which forced the plane to fly at low altitude over Portugal while dissidents dropped leaflets denouncing the regime's atrocities (Santos, 2011).

The 1960s witnessed a new wave of uprisings around the world. In Portugal these coincided with the beginning of the Colonial War in Africa in 1961, the growth of internal instability after Caetano succeeded Salazar in 1968, and increasing awareness of revolutionary activity in other countries (Leitão and Pina, 1975). These circumstances strongly influenced and intensified the political opposition in Portugal, exacerbating anti-fascist, anti-capitalist, and anti-imperialist positions and precipitating demands for an end to the oppressive regime (Leitão and Pina, 1975). At that time, there was increasing support for the notion that armed struggle was the best means to overthrow the *Estado Novo*, and this view eventually challenged the traditional reformist discourse (Cruzeiro and Bebiano, 2006). Thus, in this context, three of the organisations under analysis in the present study – the LUAR, the ARA, and the BR – took up arms and launched violent assaults against the Portuguese state.

Pre-revolution wave: 1964–1974

The LUAR

It is commonly considered that the LUAR's first public manifestation occurred in 1967, when it is said that some of its members robbed a bank in the city of Figueira da Foz. However, although most of the individuals who participated in the robbery would soon form the core of the LUAR, at the time they were simply a group of exiles who were trying to secure funds to start a politically violent organisation to fight the *Estado Novo* (Santos, 2011). Nevertheless, the robbery achieved wide publicity. Newspapers, such as *Le Monde*, printed reports about it, and it generated highly positive reactions because, for the first time, a political group that was unconnected to the PCP had been able to organise and carry out an act of considerable visibility and significant impact (Marques, 2016). Not everyone in the Portuguese opposition celebrated the creation of the LUAR, however. For instance, the PCP criticised "initiatives to precipitate armed action without having created the conditions for the development of the insurrectional process" (quoted in Pimentel, 2011, p. 11). Thus, the LUAR inaugurating the insurrectional path in Portugal, departed from the policy of mass struggle preferred by the traditional opposition (Martins and Loureiro, 1980).

At the heart of the LUAR were individuals who felt frustrated by the notion of peaceful opposition to the regime and the consequences of pursuing such a struggle (e.g., arrest, torture). These individuals came from a variety of socio-political backgrounds, sharing only a strong sense of anti-fascism and a willingness to fight the regime (see Marques, 2016). In this vein, the LUAR's militants tended to have few discussions about ideology or politics. For instance, they rarely debated the Colonial War issue (Mortágua, 2013).

However, the organisation's members had personal views and "each element recruited in the opposition political milieux brought his own pretensions of making the LUAR the 'armed wing' of his own or his group's ideological options" (Mortágua, 2013, p. 200). Among these groups, the most prominent were the Marxist–Leninists and the progressive Catholics, previously organised in exile, who saw in the LUAR an opportunity to act (Santos, 2011). However, the lack of a well defined ideology, strategic planning, and the Marcelist Spring led some people to walk away from the organisation.

It is equally important to highlight the LUAR's reliance on its charismatic leader, Hermínio da Palma Inácio. His activities seemed to dictate the rhythm of the organisation itself. Mortágua (2013), for instance, reports that he (Mortágua) moved to Paris and made extensive preparations for several operations, but it was only when Palma Inácio arrived that the actions were actually launched. The latter was also arrested several times, which invariably impacted on the organisation's activities, the timing of its operations, and, particularly, the recruitment of new and defection of existing members (Santos, 2011).

Finally, not all of the LUAR's activities (which are detailed in Table 1.1) were successful. In particular, Operation Matias resulted in the arrest of several militants, including Palma Inácio himself. This proved to be a powerful setback and it caused several militants to disengage from the organisation.

Thus, the LUAR's relatively small number of operations (when compared to the ARA or the BR) may be explained by a number of factors: the organisation's shortage of experienced clandestine militants; its internal fragility due to the existence of multiple perspectives and difficult decision-making; and constant, strong supression by the political police, which was felt through numerous, repeated arrests and successful infiltration of the organisation (Marques, 2016).

The ARA

The ARA, despite constituting a semi-autonomous organisation, was the armed wing of the PCP. Therefore, while it had its own board, which took independent decisions about specific actions, it followed the party's political instructions (Narciso, 2000). Although the decision to establish the ARA was

Table 1.1 The LUAR's armed actions

Action	*Year*	*Goal*
Operation Diana	1967	Collect weapons from the military quarter of Évora.
Operation Matias	1968	Establish control over the city of Covilhã.
Operation Spring	1969	Sabotage high-voltage pylons and plant explosives in the US Consulate in Oporto.

taken as early as 1964, its revolutionary activity only began in 1970 (Marques, 2016). This delay was due to various factors, such as the need for rigorous and time-consuming preparations, the existence of strong political repression that needed to be countered, and some uncertainty within the PCP. The latter was related to the existence of divergent views within the party concerning the armed struggle, with members generally categorised either as supporters of armed operations to weaken the regime or as supporters of the traditional peaceful mass struggle in accordance with the Soviet Union's directives (Narciso, 2000).

The ARA had a central command composed of three PCP militants, all of whom lived in the Lisbon area. However, other militants, both men and women, contributed to the carrying out of actions at various levels – technical, financial, logistical and operational (Serra, 1999). As an organisation, the ARA was extremely careful due to the strong repression and persecution perpetrated by the political police. For instance, all discussions and decision-making were restricted to the central command, which would then issue instructions to the individual militants who were to undertake specific actions (Serra, 1999).

The ARA was equally rigorous in regard to its principles and rules of operation. Its aim was to engender violent action against

> the fascist State apparatus and against the Colonial War machine, in order to psychologically weaken and disorient it, thereby stimulating the struggle of the Portuguese people for the overthrow of fascism, and the struggle of the colonial people for their liberation.
>
> (Serra, 1999, p. 29)

In terms of its armed actions, the ARA preferred to target structures that were related to the Colonial War (Serra, 1999; see Table 1.2). Moreover, along with the LUAR and the BR, it was careful to minimise the risk to human life during its operations, for instance by detonating explosives only in empty spaces (Narciso, 2000).

Ultimately, the ARA decided to suspend its operations in May 1973 (Ferreira, 2015). This decision was motivated by a desire to reduce the strong repression of the general political anti-dictatorship movement (e.g., progressive Catholics who were organising peaceful demonstrations against the Colonial War). The latter movement was gaining ground at the time, and eleven months later it would launch the revolution of 25 April 1974 (Rosas and Brito, 1996). The April Revolution and the establishment of democracy allowed the ARA to lay down its arms for good, and its members soon started to integrate into the new political life of the country.

The BR

The BR was formed in 1970 in the wake of a political rupture with the PCP (Marques, 2016). Some militants felt the need to break away from the party's

Table 1.2 The ARA's armed actions

Target	*Date*	*Goal*
Cunene	25/10/1970	Sabotage the ship *Cunene* in order to disrupt the transport of troops to the Colonial War.
Tancos Air Base	8/03/1971	Attack Air Base Number 3 in Tancos to destroy helicopters and other aircraft that would be used in the Colonial War.
Telephone and Telecommunications Centre	3/06/1971	Sabotage high-voltage pylons and plant explosives in the US Consulate in Oporto.
Power cut in Sacavém and Belas	3/06/1971	Sabotage the electricity grid.
Stone quarry storeroom	3/10/1971	Seize explosives.
NATO headquarters, Oeiras	30/10/1971	Sabotage.
Cais da Fundição	20/11/1971	Destroy war equipment.
Training college of the political police	20/11/1971	Detonate an explosive device.
US Cultural Centre	20/11/1971	Detonate an explosive device.
Muxima	25/01/1972	Destroy war materiel destined for shipment to the Colonial War on the ocean liner *Muxima*.
Electrical grid	10/08/1972	Sabotage the electricity grid in four different parts of the country.

pacifist stance and show the Portuguese people that it was possible to fight the regime (Carmo, 1974). Their resolution strengthened as disillusionment with the Marcelist Spring started to grow. In particular, they resented the electoral campaign and process of 1969, which had generated reformist illusions for a time but they ultimately opted for continuity (Sousa, 2006).

Thus, the BR represented a new way of confronting the regime, one that rejected the PCP's Stalinism and proposed armed action to achieve a socialist revolution by which means the proletariat would seize power (Antunes, 1974). In this sense, the BR always pointed to the need for a revolutionary structure of the proletariat in which the armed struggle and the mass struggle could converge (Carmo, 1974). The former was not considered more important than the latter; in fact, it was seen as the trigger to a revolutionary organisation of class (Antunes, 1974). Thus, in 1973, the PRP (Proletariat Revolutionary Party) was founded in Portugal's political underground. This party consisted of a number of militants who were united by their anti-fascist, anti-capitalist, and anti-reformist viewpoints (Goulart, 2002).

The BR's main aims were outlined in its first communiqué, dated 1971, and developed in its sixth communiqué, dated 6 April 1973. They included: the struggle against capitalism and the fascist state; the struggle against colonialism and neo-colonialism; the struggle against imperialism; the struggle against reformism and legalism; the clandestine organisation of the workers; and fusing the armed struggle with the revolutionary mass movement.

In terms of armed actions, similarly to the ARA, the BR generally attacked structures that served the Colonial War and always attempted to minimise the risk its operations posed to human life (Carmo, 2012; see Table 1.3). Unlike the ARA, the BR did undertake several bank robberies, which provided the sole means of financial support for the organisation (Ferreira, 2015). Moreover, it was "the only armed organisation which arrived at the revolution in a position of open war against the fascist regime" (Antunes, 1974, p. 12). After the April Revolution, the BR started to pursue full integration with the PRP. However, the passing of a Disarmament Law, which obliged all Portuguese citizens to surrender their weapons, prompted new underground activity in order to safeguard against the possibility of right-wing provocation or abuse of power (Partido Revolucionário do Proletariado, 1975).

Table 1.3 The BR's armed actions

Target	*Date*	*Goal*
NATO installations, Fonte da Telha	7/11/1971	Attack to display solidarity towards people of the colonies.
Barreiro	12/11/1971	Destroy a cannon battery.
Central and southern Portugal	11/05/1972	Attempt to initiate a widespread power cut.
Stone quarry between Loulé and Boliqueime, the Algarve	11/06/1972	Seize hundreds of kilograms of explosives.
Various locations	11/07/1972	Sabotage 15 Berliet army trucks.
Palmela and Sesimbra	25/08/1972	Sabotage facilities that allowed telegraphic and telephonic communications between Portugal and the colonies.
Cartographic Army Services	December 1972	Assault to seize maps of the colonies and pass them to liberation movements (PAIGC, MPLA, and FRELIMO).
Various army installations	9–10/03/1973 and 6/04/1973	Sabotage missions to disrupt the Portuguese military.
Ministry of Corporations, Lisbon	1/05/1073	Sabotage various departments.
General Military Quarter, Oporto	26/10/1973	Detonate explosives to destroy archives and building sites.
General Quarter of Guinea, Bissau	22/02/1974	Sabotage.
Niassa	9/04/1974	Sabotage the ocean liner *Niassa* to disrupt the transportation of troops to Bissau.

The April Revolution

The revolution of 25 April 1974 was the last leftist revolution in Europe, bringing an end to one of the lengthiest dictatorships of the twentieth century (Rezola, 2007). At the micro-level, such a revolution is often considered to be totally unexpected, as Narciso (2000), Santos (2011), and Mortágua (2013) explain in their memoirs. However, a macro-analysis indicates many signs of a regime marked by deep crisis, particularly in its last decade, such as:

1. The Catholic Church, one of the main pillars of the regime, promoted various actions against the Colonial War. This was influenced by Pope Paul VI himself, who in 1970 received a group of representatives from the Portuguese colonies' liberation movements, throwing into question the validity of the regime's position (Cruzeiro and Bebiano, 2006).
2. In a context of industrialisation, war, and forced exile, urban students and young workers were increasingly politicised, influenced by extreme-left ideologies, and targeted by a violent, repressive state apparatus (Cruzeiro and Bebiano, 2006; Loff, 2006).
3. The Colonial War, which began in Angola in 1961 and spread to Mozambique and Guinea-Bissau, was draining the armed forces (Rezola, 2007).
4. Portuguese citizens in the colonies started protesting against both the regime and the armed forces, which were unable to protect them from violent attacks perpetrated by the liberation movements (Rezola, 2007).
5. The international community's pressure on the regime was re-energised by the Catholic priest Adrian Hastings' denunciation of the Wiriyamu massacre in Mozambique (Hastings, 1973).
6. The armed forces' attempted coup in March 1974 (Rezola, 2007).
7. The economic difficulties Portugal was facing, particularly due to the Colonial War and the oil crisis of 1973 (Rezola, 2007).

Therefore, Portugal could be likened to a "pressure cooker" – ready to explode either of its own volition or with some encouragement (Pimentel, 2011, p. 22). Indeed, that encouragement soon arrived, albeit from an unexpected quarter: the armed forces.

The year 1973 saw the creation and consolidation of the *Movimento dos Capitães* (Captains' Movement; later renamed the *Movimento das Forças Armadas* (MFA) – Armed Forces Movement). This resulted from discontent among the military in the face of the policies of Caetano's government, namely the continuation of the Colonial War. In addition, in February 1974, General Spínola, who at the time was deputy chief of the General Staff, published *Portugal e o Futuro* (*Portugal and the Future*), in which he stated that a political rather than an armed solution to the Colonial War had to be found, primarily through recognition of the colonial people's right to self-determination (Spínola, 1974). This stance, adopted by such an important figure, triggered the regime's implosion. Spínola was dismissed, but that merely prompted the young captains to revolt.

Thus, it could be said that, from the moment when the Captains' Movement was founded, a significant part of the military connected to General Spínola started to plan the military coup which eventually took place on 25 April 1974. The coup quickly became a social revolution among the Portuguese people, who flooded onto the streets to show their support for the armed forces and demand an end to the regime. These people were subsequently able to participate in the "transitional process towards a fully institutionalised democracy" that concluded in April 1976 with the introduction of Portugal's new constitution (Loff, 2014, p. 3).

The April Revolution prompted deep structural transformations throughout the country, particularly in the economic, social and cultural spheres (Rezola, 2007). However, it also triggered new waves of armed opposition. These were launched by the ELP and the MDLP in 1975, and subsequently by the FP-25 in 1980.

The return of politically motivated violence

The waves of post-revolution violence were triggered by the extreme right's and the extreme left's opposition, in different periods as it will be explained, to the changes introduced by the democratic process. The first wave started in the summer of 1975, during the period known as the *Processo Revolucionário em Curso* (PREC) – the Ongoing Revolutionary Process. It was motivated by a belief, held by conservative and pro-*Estado Novo* individuals, that the April Revolution had opened the door to the implementation of a "Marxist/Communist/collectivist/totalitarian dictatorship worse than Salazar's" (Loff, 2014, p. 2). According to Kenneth Maxwell (1999), this belief was strengthened by various developments:

1. The active participation of the PCP in the political and administrative organisation of the country.
2. The strong divergences between General Spínola (who had been installed as president of the Republic), the PCP, and the MFA, especially in relation to the colonies.
3. Spínola's resignation, which weakened the conservative and reformist forces in the transitional process and allowed the colonies to assert their independence.
4. A failed "anti-communist" coup on 11 March 1975, led by Spínola, which contributed to the radicalisation of the MFA.
5. The nationalisation of banks, insurance companies, and private property.

It was in this context that popular anti-communist violence erupted in the so-called *Verão Quente* (Hot Summer) of 1975, particularly in the rural northern and central regions of Portugal, which were dominated by Catholic landowners. These landowners did not welcome the socialist proposals of the Revolutionary Council. In some cases, they even answered the call of counter-revolution organisations to display their dissatisfaction by attacking PCP headquarters (Cerezales, 2003). Simultaneously, the ELP and the MDLP, two armed organisations composed of conservative individuals who had fled into exile in Spain after the unsuccessful coup of 11 March 1975, attempted to orchestrate popular unrest against left-wing individuals and organisations within Portugal. In the midst of a clearly divided world, characterised by the polarising rivalries of the Cold War and a nation on the brink of civil war, the ELP and the MDLP believed that they would be able "to invade the country and defeat the communists by force of arms" (Dâmaso, 1997, p. 11).

This very troubled period in Portugal's political history came to an end on 25 November 1975, when forces loyal to Colonel Ramalho Eanes' repulsed an attempted coup by some extreme-left troops, thereby facilitating the development of an institutionalised democratic regime (Maxwell, 1999). Therefore, 25 November 1975 marked the end of the extreme right's armed offensive (Dâmaso, 1997). However, it simultaneously laid the foundations for a new wave of political violence, this time conducted by the extreme left (Costa, 2004).

The counter-revolution wave: 1975–1976

The ELP

When Marcelo Caetano superseded Salazar as prime minister in 1968, irreconcilable differences opened between the conventional right, which supported the new leader, and the so-called ultra or orthodox right, composed of intellectual nationalists. The latter group accused *Marcelismo* of: extreme superficiality in terms of politics and ideology; ignoring their presence and opinions; and allowing left-wing activities and ultimately the April Revolution, which they viewed as a disastrous event in Portuguese history (Dugos, 1976). Before the revolution, the ultra right held multiple political demonstrations and gatherings, published a number of newspapers, and forged close links with other anti-communist movements around the world. Through these activities, it continued to recruit ever more young militants. After the revolution, many right-wingers organised themselves in various legitimate political parties (e.g., the Liberal Party, the Progress Party, the Independent Republicans, the Christian Democrats) and participated in the democratic process. However, others felt that traditional political parties were unable to fight the growth of communism in the new democracy. This feeling was exacerbated by an attack on the Progress Party's headquarters in September 1974 and by the police's persecution of a number of that organisation's militants (Dugos, 1976). In response, Barbieri Cardoso, a former sub-director of the *Estado Novo*'s political police, founded the ELP in January 1975. The new organisation consisted of supporters of the deposed regime, including former members of the Portuguese Legion and the political police (Matos, 2005), and it garnered support among elements of the Spanish secret services and European neo-fascist refugees living in Spain (Marchi, 2012). The members of the ELP dwelt in the political underground and adopted a military configuration. According to Carlos Dugos (1976), who interviewed the organisation's leaders in Spain, the ELP aimed to: restore national unity, which had been jeopardised by the "Marxist" revolution; re-establish genuine Portuguese independence, which was threatened by global communism; and reassert cultural freedom, which had been subjugated by Marxist dogmatism.

In regard to the colonial issue, the ELP took an integrationist approach by advocating the permanent integration of the colonies within national territory. This would mean the eradication of the long-standing differences between Portugal and its colonies, and the annihilation of the colonies' liberation movements through force of arms (Dugos, 1976).

The organisation had militants in various countries – Portugal itself, Spain, France, Germany, Angola, South Africa, and Brazil – and received financial support from Portuguese small and medium-sized business owners, emigrants, and other sympathisers (Dugos, 1976). It carried out its first operation in May 1975, when some of its members attacked the PCP's Work Centre in Bragança. This marked the start of the aforementioned Hot Summer of 1975 and introduced Portugal to the organisation's acronym, which would become extremely visible throughout the country over the next few months (Cerqueira, 2015). Thereafter, numerous other bombings and attacks on PCP headquarters were attributed to the ELP.

The MDLP

The MDLP also emerged from the ultra right which opposed *Marcelismo.* It was presided over by General Spínola (now in exile in Brazil) and simultaneously led in Spain by Alpoim Calvão (Hortelão, Baêna and Sousa, 2012). The MDLP was considered less radical in its views than the ELP. For instance, its militants believed that the time for authoritarian regimes was over and that the future belonged to a democratic right-wing government (Dugos, 1976). Nevertheless, they agreed that counter-revolutionary measures were needed "to prevent the establishment of a communist regime or Marxist military dictatorship in Portugal; and to create the conditions for the implementation of a free and pluralistic democratic system" (untitled MDLP document, 1975, cited in Hortelão *et al.*, 2012, p. 372). Consequently, the MDLP envisaged a democratic Portugal in which all political parties, aside from left-wing ones, would have a place.

Its armed activities began in May 1975 and officially ended in November of that year. Although short-lived, they included the detonation of explosive devices, particularly against the PCP's headquarters (Dâmaso, 1997). Therefore, throughout the Hot Summer of 1975, it was difficult to distinguish between the two organisations that were engaging in armed struggle because they were attacking the same targets – communist political structures and individuals – and both appealing for support from the population in the north. One MDLP flyer read:

> When you hear the bells ringing in your parish, come to the street with the weapons you have: shotguns, pistols, picks, hoes and scythes ... There is an urgent need to prepare to unleash, all over Portugal, a white crusade against the red oppression, against foreign communism, the godless usurper and oppressor.
>
> (Cited in Hortelão *et al.*, 2012, pp. 377–378)

The MDLP's operations were funded by supporters in various countries, including Spain, France, the United Kingdom, Angola, Zaire, South Africa, Rhodesia, Mozambique, Brazil, Venezuela, the United States, and Canada. The group attracted particular attention in the United States, where there was considerable concern over the possible establishment of a communist state in Portugal (Dâmaso, 1997).

In regard to the colonial issue, the MDLP adopted a federalist approach in that it hoped to create a cultural, political, economic, and linguistic federation of the colonies (Dugos, 1976). This approach was based on ideas presented by Spínola in *Portugal and the Future*.

Following the defeat of the extreme left on 25 November 1975, the leaders of the MDLP could not envisage a future for the organisation, so they set about dismantling it (Marchi, 2012). However, not everyone within the MDLP agreed with this decision. Some militants continued to plant bombs, "some in revenge against the communists, others for money, turning into a spiral of violence that quickly evolved into a more or less sophisticated form of terrorism" (Dâmaso, 1997, p. 20).

The post-revolution wave: 1980–1987

The FP-25

The FP-25, created in 1980, was formed by left-wing radical activists who were disappointed by the socio-political path that Portugal had followed since 25 November 1975. From their perspective, this had led to serious social injustice, especially in the workplace (Costa, 2004). Several FP-25 activists had previously organised in the context of the PRP/BR, and they were motivated to join the new group for two distinct reasons, as explained by Manuel Ricardo de Sousa (1992). Some individuals did not agree with setting aside their weapons after the April Revolution because they believed that an armed struggle would still be necessary to attain a socialist revolution. Others felt that their only option was to remain underground because they had participated in bank robberies to fund the PRP/BR.

According to José Barra da Costa (2004), the FP-25 was the armed wing of the *Projecto Global* (Global Project), created in 1979 by Otelo Saraiva de Carvalho, one of the revolution's army captains. The Global Project's main goals were: prevention of a fascist *coup d'état*; creation of the necessary conditions to seize power; establishment of popular power; and consequent changes to the operation of state institutions. It consisted of a number of legal political structures in addition to its clandestine component, the FP-25. The latter group was designed to fight the extreme right, which was perceived to be regaining power and was certainly launching violent attacks against the left (see Ventura and Nascimento, 2001). The militants used this as justification to take matters into their own hands and commit themselves to the revolutionary struggle.

The FP-25's militants, who were divided among small cells in various locations around the country, used guns or explosive devices in the course of several assassination attempts (Costa, 2004). According to António Vilela (2005), such actions mainly targeted factory owners or administrators who were seen as abusive towards their employees, for example by delaying the payment of wages or initiating unjustified redundancies. Hence, the members of the FP-25 were able to claim that they supported the working class. They also carried out several bank robberies and targeted a handful of police officers, the director of the Prison Service and ex-militants who had collaborated with the authorities. Indeed, it is impossible to cover the full range of the FP-25's missions in detail here. Nevertheless, Table 1.4 gives some impression of the depth and breadth of the organisation's activities.

The police started the process of dismantling the FP-25 with the help of three collaborators in 1983. The following June, the *Polícia Judiciária* (Portugal's criminal investigation police service), in conjunction with the Public Ministry (the country's Public Prosecution Service), arrested eighty people during Operation Orion (Ventura, 1999). Most of the remaining members were arrested or fled abroad between 1985 and 1987, and the FP-25 finally ceased all operations in 1989.

From October 1986 onwards, a total of eighty-seven defendants faced trials over offences relating to FP-25 activities, but it would be many more years before the whole judicial process was completed, as Loff (2015) explains. In December 1991, seven FP-25 detainees were granted presidential pardons; in March 1996, Parliament passed an amnesty for several imprisoned members of the organisation; and, in April 2001, sixty defendants were acquitted of all charges relating to homicides committed by the FP-25 due to a lack of evidence (these cases had not been included in the 1996 amnesty).

The post-April Revolution: political violence and memory politics

These voices and stories of former politically violent militants have been recurrently silenced in the Portuguese "battle over memory" because their activities were linked to events, such as the April Revolution, which themselves have been politically and socially depreciated in mainstream political narratives (Loff, 2014, p. 10).

Table 1.4 The FP-25's armed actions

Target	*Date*	*Justification and/or outcome*
Totta & Açores Bank and Crédito Predial Português	05/05/1980	Bank robberies and murder of a police officer (Henrique do Nascimento Hipólito).
Civil Registry Office	22/07/1980	Theft of twenty identity cards.
Director, Standard Eléctrica	23/08/1981	Response to layoffs and labour disputes. The target and his driver received gunshot wounds to the legs and chest.
Administrator, Louças de Sacavém	6/12/1982	The company had a record of unpaid wages, which had resulted in a number of workers' protests. The target (Diamantino Monteiro Pereira) was killed.
Branches of Espírito Santo Bank, Caldas da Raínha and Leiria	3/12/1983	Detonation of explosives at two separate sites in solidarity with the workers of CIVE, a company that the bank refused to support financially, resulting in unemployment and unpaid wages.
Administrator, Ivima	25/01/1984	The company was in the midst of a dispute with its workers. Several shots were fired at the at the house of the target (Jorge Raposo Magalhães) and a Molotov cocktail was left on his doorstep.
Businessmen, Covilhã and Castelo Branco	28/02/1984	Detonation of car bombs targeting several businessmen accused of poor labour relations.
Landowner, São Manços	30/04/1984	Detonation of an explosive device against an outer wall of the landowner's house. A four-month-old baby (Nuno Dionísio) was killed.
Administrator, Gelmar	29/05/1984	Gelmar had unjustly fired employees and the administrator in question, Canha e Sá, was held responsible for its bankruptcy, as well as those of other companies where he had worked. He was killed in the attack.
Rosa Barradas	19/07/1985	Former militant, killed for collaborating with the police.
Gaspar Castelo Branco, General Manager of the Prison Service	15/02/1986	Response to the harsh conditions in which FP-25 militants were detained and to the alleged intransigence of the Prison Service. The target was killed.
The police	16/08/1987	Gunfire between the police and the FP-25, which resulted in the death of one police officer (Álvaro Militão).

The counter-revolution that took place on 25 November 1975 brought to an end the revolutionary phase of the transition to democracy. Thus, the Ongoing *Revolutionary* Process was superseded by the Ongoing *Constitutional* Process (Cruzeiro, 2005). The counter-revolution also signalled the defeat of radical leftist organisations and movements in Portugal (Cerqueira 2015). This defeat was cemented by the left's poor displays in the constitutional election of 1975 and the presidential election of 1976. Thereafter, the establishment of representative democracy in Portugal could begin in earnest. In this context, the triumphant political sectors sought to halt and defuse the revolutionary transformations that had occurred over the previous two years (e.g., agrarian reform and various nationalisations), even though they were constitutionally consecrated (Rosas, 2004). This new framework, the herald of political stability, allowed Portugal to submit a formal application to join the European Economic Community (EEC) in March 1977.

The institutionalisation of democracy was accompanied by an effort to create an atmosphere of reconciliation in Portuguese society by discouraging condemnation and providing amnesties for those who had engaged in armed violence from both the far right and the far left of the political spectrum (Camacho, 2011). Moreover, the political project of the neoconservative and economically neoliberal Cavaco Silva, prime minister between 1985 and 1995, required the rejection of the April Revolution as a historical experience. It was at this point that various scholars and politicians started denying the categorisation of the *Estado Novo* as "fascist". They adopted an authoritarian, non-totalitarian and non-fascist perspective, while recurrently depicting the April Revolution as highly negative. Hence, a "negative perception of the Revolution and of the democratic system built upon it apparently concealed the negative memories of Salazar's regime" (Loff, 2014, p. 6). In this context, one of the most striking ways in which such memories were concealed was through the blocking of access, until 1996, to Salazar's personal and political archives, as well as those of the political police. These aspects, then, laid the foundation for the reconfiguration of memory discourses and of memory politics, creating political narratives that deliberately devalued memories of the anti-fascist resistance and the April Revolution, and rewrote more recent history in an objective process of historical revisionism (Rosas, 2016).

However, in the 1990s, public debates concerned with the "sheer whitewashing of the dictatorship" by right-wing governments began to take place, starting a "rebellion of memory" (Loff, 2014, p. 10). This period also witnessed the beginning of a new political cycle marked by the Socialist Party's accession to power. Hence, on its twenty-fifth anniversary, for the first time, the April Revolution was celebrated with enthusiasm by the political establishment. At this point, a stimulus was provided for the publication of autobiographical accounts and memoirs by some of the militants who had participated in the resistance against the dictatorship. As they entered old age, they became aware of the need to redress the autobiographical narrative, since they found themselves confronted by a proliferation of revisionist discourses, which denied Portugal's repressive past. Thus, from the turn of the century onwards, several former militants decided to write and publish their memoirs and the "histories" of their respective organisations (e.g., Serra, 1999; Narciso, 2000; Santos, 2011; Hortelão *et al.*, 2012; Mortágua, 2013; Marques, 2016; Carmo, 2017). Some family members (e.g. Lindim, 2012) and academics (e.g., Vilela, 2005; Cardina, 2011; Pimentel, 2014) followed suit. However, some of these books (e.g., Narciso, 2000; Lindim, 2012) still used pseudonyms because former militants continued to fear discrimination in their social circles (e.g., among family and friends or in the workplace).

The return to power of the right-wing in 2002 influenced the celebrations of the thirtieth anniversary of the April Revolution two years later. Once again, the governmental elite was concerned by the revolutionary legacy. The official slogan of the celebrations – "April is Evolution" (rather than Revolution) – provoked a strong reaction in the media and the public sphere. The right-wing strategy of imposing an evolutionary character on the April Revolution, in tune with the idea of transition, was shattered by the political reaction in defence of the revolution as a specifically Portuguese model of building democracy (Loff, 2015).

During the difficult years of the recent economic crisis (2011–2015), which mainly affected the middle and lower classes, there was significant memory recovery regarding the more radical forms of struggle. In the face of a general lack of hope, the apparent ineffectiveness of peaceful demonstrations, the deaf ears of politicians, a discourse of inevitability, and a sense of powerlessness to change personal circumstances, a political narrative linked to the need for a violent response to reverse the situation once again emerged. However, the recalled violence focused primarily on the pre-revolution period, when the struggle against the dictatorship and the Colonial War, and the fact that blood crimes were not committed, seemed to justify a degree of sympathy towards political violence. In this sense, the armed activities committed throughout the counter- and post-revolution periods started to fall into oblivion. The country went through a democratisation process and the existence of political violence under democracy became an unspoken aspect of the history of armed struggle in Portugal.

Conclusion

This chapter has outlined the historical context in which armed organisations emerged, acted, and dissolved in various periods in Portugal. This context is fundamental to our understanding of the narratives of political violence that are explored in the rest of this book – narratives that are presented by individuals who invested significant years of their lives fighting violently for their political ideals.

I delineated three historical periods (pre-, counter- and post-revolution waves) in which politically motivated violence occurred in Portugal. Each of these historical periods was characterised by certain socio-political developments which led to armed operations by both left- and right-wing militants. In Chapter 3, I will demonstrate how contextual perceptions shaped individual militants' identities in ways that influenced their engagement with politically violent organisations.

In this chapter, I have also argued that former militants' voices and experiences have been silenced due to the whitewashing of the *Estado Novo* regime and the consequent historical revisionism which took root in Portugal from the late 1970s until the early 1990s. I have demonstrated how part of Portugal's historical identity has been manipulated by political and ideological interests and motivations, and in turn this process has influenced the nation's collective memory. However, I have also demonstrated that memory has become an intense cultural and political battlefield since the 1990s. All sides have made efforts to tell their stories, broadening the nation's political narratives. I see this book as part of these efforts.

In the following chapter, I introduce my conceptual and analytical frameworks, and explain how combining the core elements of Critical Terrorism Studies with a narrative approach influenced the way in which I conducted the research for this book. I also unpack and exemplify the main principles behind the DST, which are applied across the analytical Chapters 3, 4, and 5. Finally, I describe how I embarked on a process of data co-construction with the interviewees, as well as my method of data analysis.

References

Albuquerque, A. (1987) *Stress – causas, prevenção e controlo – um guia prático.* Lisbon: Informação e Saúde, Texto Editora.

Alves, V. M. (1997) 'Os etnógrafos locais e o secretariado da propaganda nacional', *Etnográfica*, 1, pp. 237–257.

Amaro, R. (1982) 'O salazarismo na lógica do capitalism em Portugal', *Análise Social*, 18(72–74), pp. 995–1011.

Antunes, C. (1974) *Dossier Brigadas Revolucionárias.* Lisbon: Edições Revolução.

Baiôa, M. (1994) 'A ditadura militar na historiografia recente', *Penélope*, 14, pp. 201–217.

Barreto, J. (2000) 'Tarrafal', in Barreto, A. and Mónica, F. (eds) *Dicionário de história de Portugal – suplemento, Volume IX.* Oporto: Figueirinhas, pp. 486–490.

Cabrera, A. (2014) 'A memória e o esquecimento: a censura do Estado Novo em Portugal perante três peças de autores espanhóis', *Revista eletrónica de teoria da literatura e literatura comparada*, 10, pp. 89–110. Available at: www.452f.com/pdf/numero10/10_452f-mono-ana-cabrera-orgnl.pdf (accessed 20/04/2018).

Camacho, J. (2011) *Terrorismo em Portugal, a guerra esquecida.* Self-published.

Cardina, M. (2010) 'Política , Ppunição e silenciamento nas oposições radicais ao *Estado Novo*', *O Cabo dos Trabalhos: Revista Electrónica dos Programas de Mestrado e Doutoramento do CES/ FEUC/ FLUC*, 4, pp. 12–16. Available at: http://cabodostrabalhos.ces.uc.pt/pdf/18_Miguel_Cardina.pdf (accessed 20/04/2018).

Cardina, M. (2011) *Margem de certa maneira: o Maoismo em Portugal (1964–1974).* Lisbon: Tinta da China.

Carmo, I. (1974) 'A violência no processo revolucionário', *Revolução*, 1, p. 6.

Carmo, I. (2012) 'As mulheres nas Brigadas Revolucionárias', in Lindim, I. (ed.) *Mulheres de armas: história das Brigadas Revolucionárias – as acções armadas, os riscos, as motivações*. Carnaxide: Editora Objectiva, pp. 13–72.

Carmo, I. (2017) *A luta armada*. Lisbon: Dom Quixote.

Cerezales, D. P. (2003) 'Um caso de violência política: o "verão quente"', *Análise Social*, 37(165), pp. 1127–1157.

Cerqueira, A. (2015) *Revolução e contra-revolução em Portugal (1974–1975)*. Lisbon: Parsifal.

Collotti, E. (1989) *Fascismo, fascismi*. Firenze: Sansoni.

Costa, J. (2004) *O terrorismo e as FP-25 anos depois*. Lisbon: Edições Colibri.

Cruzeiro, M. (2005) *25 de Novembro: quantos golpes afinal?* Available at: http://www1.ci.uc.pt/cd25a/wikka.php?wakka=th10 (accessed 20/04/2018).

Cruzeiro, M. and Bebiano, R. (2006) *Anos inquietos: vozes do movimento estudantil em Coimbra (1961–1974)*. Oporto: Edições Afrontamento.

Dâmaso, E. (1997) *A invasão Spinolista*. Lisbon: Fenda.

Dugos, C. (1976) *MDLP – ELP – o que são?*Lisbon: Edições Acrópole.

Ferreira, A. S. (2015) *Luta armada em Portugal (1970–1974)*. Universidade Nova de Lisboa. Available at: https://run.unl.pt/handle/10362/16326 (accessed 20/04/2018).

Ferro, A. (1982) *Salazar: o homem e a sua obra*. Lisbon: Fernando Pereira Edições.

Fonseca, T. (2005) *'Introdução' a livros proibidos no Estado Novo*. Lisbon: Divisão de Edições da Assembleia da República.

Gama, M. (2008) *Da censura à autocensura no Estado Novo*. Braga: Universidade do Minho.

Goulart, P. (2002) *Resistência*. Lisbon: Edições Dinossauro.

Hastings, A. (1973) *Wiriyamu*. London: Search Press.

Hortelão, R., Baêna, L. and Sousa, A. (2012) *Alpoim Calvão: honra e dever*. Oporto: Caminhos Romanos.

Kayman, M. (1987) *Revolution and counter-revolution in Portugal*. London: Merlin.

Leitão, F. and Pina, C. (1975) *LUAR: o que é?*Lisbon: Agência Portuguesa de Revistas.

Lindim, I. (2012) *Mulheres de armas: história das Brigadas Revolucionárias – as acções armadas, os riscos, as motivações*. Carnaxide: Editora Objectiva.

Loff, M. (2006) 'Fim do colonialismo, ruptura política e transformação social em Portugal nos assos setenta', in Loff, M. and Pereira, M. da C. M. (eds) *Portugal, 30 anos de democracia (1974–2004)*. Oporto: Editora da UP, pp. 153–193.

Loff, M. (2014) 'Dictatorship and revolution: socio-political reconstructions of collective memory in post-authoritarian Portugal', *Culture and History*, 3(2), pp. 1–13.

Loff, M. (2015) 'Estado, democracia e memória: políticas públicas da memória da ditadura portuguesa (1974–2004)', in Loff, M., Soutelo, L. and Piedade, F. (eds) *Ditaduras e revolução: democracia e políticas da memória*. Coimbra: Almedina, pp. 23–144.

Lucena, M. de (1979) 'The evolution of Portuguese corporatism under Salazar and Caetano', in Graham, L. S. and Makler, H. M. (eds) *Contemporary Portugal: the revolution and its antecedents*. Austin: University of Texas Press, pp. 47–88.

Marchi, R. (2012) 'A extrema-direita portuguesa na "Rua": da transição à democracia (1976–1980)', *Locus, Revista de História, Juíz de Fora*, 18(1), pp. 167–186.

Marques, F. P. (2016) *Uma nova concepção da luta*. Lisbon: Tinta da China.

Martins, J. and Loureiro, R. (1980) 'As organizações armadas em Portugal de 1967 a 1974', *História*, 18, pp. 14–26.

Matos, A. (2005) 'Nomes, siglas e casos para entender um ano decisivo', *Diário de Notícias*. Available at: www.dn.pt/inicio/interior.aspx?content_id=620611&page=-1 (accessed 20/04/2018).

Maxwell, K. (1999) *A construção da democracia em Portugal*. Lisbon: Editorial Presença.

Mortágua, C. (2013) *Andanças para a liberdade, Volume II: 1961–1974*. Lisbon: Esfera do Caos.

Narciso, R. (2000) *ARA – Acção Revolucionária Armada: a história secreta do braço armado do PCP*. Lisbon: Dom Quixote.

Nolte, E. (1966) *The three faces of fascism: Action Française, Italian Fascism, National Socialism*. New York: Holt, Rinehart and Winston.

Oliveira, C. (1990) 'A evolução política', in Marques, A. O. and Serrão, J. (eds) *Nova história de Portugal, Volume XII: Portugal e o Estado Novo (1930–1960)*. Lisbon: Editorial Presença, pp. 21–85.

Oliveira, G. (1987) *Memória viva do Tarrafal*. Lisbon: Edições Avante.

Partido Revolucionário do Proletariado (1975) *Manifesto contra a guerra civil: insurreição armada*. Lisbon: PRP.

Pimentel, I. (2007) 'A tortura', in Madeira, J., Farinha, L. and Pimentel, I. (eds) *Vítimas de Salazar: Estado Novo e violência política*. Lisbon: A Esfera dos Livros, pp. 105–127.

Pimentel, I. (2011) 'Prefácio', in Hipólito Santos, J. (ed.) *Felizmente houve a LUAR*. Lisbon: Editora Âncora, pp. 7–24.

Pimentel, I. (2014) *História da oposição à ditadura Portugesa: 1926–1974*. Oporto: Figueirinhas.

Pinto, A. C. (1999) 'Le Salazarisme e le fascism européen', *Vingtième Siècle, Revue d'histoire*, 62(1), pp. 15–25.

Pinto, A. C. (2012) *The nature of fascism revisited*. New York: SSM/Columbia University Press.

Pinto, A. C. and Rezola, M. I. (2007) 'Political Catholicism, crisis of democracy and Salazar's New State in Portugal', *Totalitarian Movements and Poltiical Religions*, 8 (2), pp. 353–368.

Raby, D. (1988) *A resistência antifascista em Portugal: comunistas, democratas e militares em oposição a Salazar, 1941-1974*. Lisbon: Editora Salamandra.

Ramos, R., Sousa, B. V. and Monteiro, N. G. (2009) *História de Portugal*. Lisbon: A Esfera dos Livros.

Rezola, M. (2007) *25 de Abril: mitos de uma revolução*. Lisbon: Esfera dos Livros.

Rosas, F. (1989a) 'A crise do liberalismo e as origens do "autoritarianismo moderno" e do Estado Novo em Portugal', *Penélope*, 2, pp. 98–114.

Rosas, F. (1989b) 'Cinco pontos em torno do estudo comparado do fascismo', *Vértice* (second series), 13, pp. 21–29.

Rosas, F. (2001) 'O salazarismo e o homem novo: ensaio sobre o *Estado Novo* e a questão do totalitarismo', *Analise Social*, 35(157), pp. 1031–1054.

Rosas, F. (2004) 'Notas para um debate: a revolução e a democracia', in Rosas, F. and Louçã, F. (eds) *Ensaio geral: Passado e futuro do 25 de Abril*. Lisbon: Dom Quixote, pp. 15–49.

Rosas, F. (2016) *História e memória: 'última lição' de Fernando Rosas*. Lisbon: Tinta da China.

Rosas, F. and Brito, J. (1996) *Dicionário de história do Estado Novo*. Venda Nova: Bertrand Editora.

Rosas, F. and Oliveira, P. A. (2004) *A transição falhada: o Marcelismo e o fim do Estado Novo (1968–1974)*. Lisbon: Editorial Notícias.

Salazar, A. (1946) 'As grandes certezas da Revolução Nacional', in *Discursos e notas políticas (1935–1937), Volume II*. 2nd Edition. Coimbra: Coimbra Editora, pp. 125–147.

Santos, J. (2011) *Felizmente houve a LUAR*. Lisbon: Editora Âncora.

Serra, J. (1999) *As explosões que abalaram o fascismo: o que foi a ARA*. Lisbon: Edições Avante.

Sousa, J. (2006) *Os movimentos de libertação face à perspectiva de uma revolução em Portugal ainda nos anos 60*. Coimbra: Arquivo Electrónico do Centro de Documentação 25 de Abril, Universidade de Coimbra.

Sousa, M. R. de (1992) *Guerrilha no asfalto: as FP-25 e o tempo português*. Lisbon: Fora do Texto.

Spínola, A. (1974) *Portugal e o futuro*. 2nd Edition. Lisbon: Arcádia.

Ventura, J. (1999) 'Motivação e identidade psicossocial na afiliação terrorista: da violência política à guerra psicológica', in Gonçalves, R. (ed.) *Crimes, práticas e testemunhos*. Braga: Universidade do Minho, pp. 109–122.

Ventura, J. and Nascimento, J. (2001) 'Violência, terrorismo e psicologia: uma abordagem exploratória', *Revista Portuguesa de Ciência Criminal*, 4, pp. 633–698.

Vilela, A. (2005) *Viver e morrer em nome das FP-25*. Lisbon: Casa das Letras.

Wheeler, D. L. and Opello, W. C. (2010) *Historical dictionary of Portugal*. Lanham, MD: Scarecrow Press.

2 Identity journeys through political narratives of violence

This book is clearly steered by two paradigmatic lenses: critical theory and narrative inquiry. On the one hand, critical theory, as opposed to traditional theory, allows me to question the established knowledge about the social phenomenon under study and how such knowledge was generated (Cox, 1986, p. 208). It also allows me to "isolate and critique those rationalisations of society which are advanced as self-evident truths, but which may be ideological mystifications" (Hoffman, 1987, p. 236). Meanwhile, narrative inquiry focuses on the storied nature of human conduct (Sarbin, 1986), considering that "social reality is primarily a narrative reality" (Spector-Mersel, 2010, p. 211). According to Andrews (2007), the way in which individuals present themselves through the stories they tell encompasses their past, their present, and their imagined future, as well as the audience they are addressing and the narratives they have constructed over the years. She then goes even further and adds that personal narratives not only talk about the individual "but provide a small window into the engines of history and historical change, as we both shape and are shaped by the events of our day" (Andrews, 2007, p. 51). Therefore, at the heart of life stories, it is possible to find the intersection between historical context and personal circumstances, which sheds light on how and why certain events take place and why individuals behave in certain ways.

I have combined these paradigmatic lenses in the hope of bringing the historical, social, political, cultural, and human contextual angles back to the political violence arena. Consequently, this book looks at political violence "as a symptom of a dysfunctional social order" rather than "as a symptom of a dysfunction in the social order" (Toros, 2012, p. 21), with the aim of understanding the role played by violence within the social reality through the perspectives and experiences of its first-hand agents. Thus, it is based on the assumption that voices should be given to politically violent militants in order that we – and they – may make sense of their experiences and gain access to the contexts and narratives through which they frame their lives.

In this chapter, I first make the case for why we need to analyse the political narratives produced by former politically violent militants through critical lenses in order to understand why they engage with, remain in, and ultimately disengage from armed struggle. I then introduce a theoretical framework to capture and interpret such narratives at the micro-level, which provides in-depth information regarding the meso- and macro-level contexts in which they are created.

Why Critical Terrorism Studies?

This book is aligned with the literature generated by CTS scholars and particularly influenced by works produced in the fields of anthropology, sociology, international relations, and psychology (see, e.g., Zulaika, 1988; Sluka, 1989; Mahmood, 1996; Zulaika and Douglass, 1996; Toros, 2012; Heath-Kelly, 2013). In these fields, researchers tend to consider that the lack of primary research in the field of terrorism and the lack of context – whether historical, social, cultural, or political – create knowledge flaws, identifiable by the existence of diverse stereotypical facts and misconceptions (Gunning, 2007; Jackson, 2007). Terms such as "terrorism" and "terrorist" are perceived as unhelpful because they elevate the phenomenon to an exceptional plan when compared with other types of equally relevant politically motivated violence. They represent power relations and dehumanise the actors who are labelled "terrorists" (Toros, 2008). In this vein, in this book, I prefer to use expressions such as "political violence" and "politically violent militant" or simply "militant", rather than "terrorism" and "terrorist". Of course, this preference does not deny the importance of some invaluable research that has been conducted under the term "terrorism". Yet, by adopting an alternative idiom, I hope to encourage prejudice-free conversations with politically violent militants since, in the words of Jeffrey Sluka:

> Just as "races" do not exist in reality, but classifications of mankind do, so too terrorism, at least as presented by elites, the mainstream media, and much of orthodox terrorism studies is unreal, but the classification of this political violence as "terrorism" has real and fateful results.
>
> (Sluka, 2009, p. 154)

Indeed terrorism is never defined from a neutral angle, but always involves contextual variables which should not be ignored. These variables can be political, social, economic, cultural, or even historical in nature, and when analysed they contribute to the reconstruction of the sequence of events that surrounded violence. Such a reconstruction enables our understanding of what came before and after violence through reflection on questions about "how the violence became possible", "what impact it had on society", and "how it relates to other social practices" (Toros and Gunning, 2009, p. 94). Thus, this type of contextually rooted analysis of political violence allows a more dynamic and fluid perspective on terroristic-labelled actions and actors, recognising their place in the wider social spheres, networks and movements of activism, protest, and militancy. It also sheds light on the dynamics between the state and individuals, the state and violent organisations, individuals and violent organisations, and violent organisations and other social movements. This is an analysis that might change the actor's place in the terrorist scenario, and may place some states' actions at the origins of terrorism (Gunning, 2007), corroborating the assumption that the line between acts of terrorism and counter-terrorism is sometimes very tenuous (Jackson, 2008). Hence, in-depth accounts of political violence, which incorporate temporal and historical aspects, look at violence in the context of wider practices, and engage with violent activists as people with pasts and futures, are much more useful than mere definitions of the term "terrorism".

Therefore, CTS consist of "terrorism-related research that self-consciously adopts a sceptical attitude towards state-centric understandings of terrorism and which does not take existing terrorism knowledge for granted but is willing to challenge widely held assumptions and beliefs" (Jackson, 2007, p. 246). In this vein, Richard Jackson's "core commitments of Critical Terrorism Studies" are organised around three overarching elements: ontological, epistemological, and ethical (Jackson, 2007). In ontological terms, CTS perceive the term "terrorism" as a label that merely represents a violent political strategy that is employed by both state and non-state actors. It is also perceived as a social fact that evolves, and changes according to spatial and temporal coordinates, *not* as a stable, objective, and scientifically identifiable phenomenon. In epistemological terms, knowledge is considered a social process attained by language, discourse, and relational exercises, which is always dependent on the context of its conception and connected to power because it is susceptible to serving "as a political tool of influence and dominance" (Jackson, Jarvis, Gunning, and Smyth, 2011, p. 37). Thereby, CTS recognise the uncertainty and partiality of knowledge regarding terrorism, suggesting a clear and constant critical reflexivity in the knowledge production process. This includes acknowledging the subjectivity of the researcher, the interests behind the research, and the effects it can have on society in general. CTS equally invite methodological and disciplinary pluralism, combat ahistorical and decontextualised analysis, raise gender issues, and engage with communities and professionals in the field. In ethical terms, CTS give precedence to universal human values and societal security, rather than national security concerns. It also assumes an emancipatory approach which aims to eradicate the myths and preconceptions that surround terrorism research. Such myths incarcerate people in dynamics of fear and terror and prevent examination of the conditions that impel individuals to resort to terroristic strategies.

How Critical Terrorism Studies?

In this section, I explain how the three overarching elements within the core commitments of CTS – ontological, epistemological, and ethical – apply to this book. However, I am aware that I am diving into fine research detail in the following paragraphs. This may be relevant for students of political violence such as myself, but immaterial for other readers. Therefore, please feel free to jump ahead to the next section if what follows is of little interest.

In ontological terms, I opted for the self-reflexive minimal foundationalism proposed by CTS scholars Harmonie Toros and Jeroen Gunning (2009), which in turn has its origins in the Frankfurt School of critical theory (see Horkheimer, 1992). This approach views terrorism as a category of violence, albeit one that is historically positioned and changes over time. Consequently, self-reflexive minimal foundationalism allows for investigation of how terrorism is represented in discourse, "while at the same time retaining a category that also engages with the strategies of the violence of a conflict" (Toros, 2012, p. 29). In this vein, throughout this book, I demonstrate how former militants position themselves with respect to the armed actions they perpetrated but also with respect to the perspectives of external past, present, and future audiences, and of other organisations that are committed to armed struggle around the world. Therefore, this ontological approach creates a bridge between what Gareth Morgan and Linda Smircich (1980) considered to be objective (e.g., positivist) and subjective (e.g., post-structuralist) approaches to reality, "retaining categories of regularity while remaining aware of their contingency and political effect, and thus constantly seeking to interrogate and destabilise them" (Toros and Gunning, 2009, p. 93). However, it is important to note that despite differentiating phenomena according to their characteristics, such an ontological perspective also acknowledges that these characteristics and their interpretation are context-bound rather than positivist objective facts. In this sense, I also demonstrate the "relative ontological insecurity of analytical concepts" proposed by critical scholars (Jackson, 2015, p. 25). They consider terms such as "terrorism", "conflict", "violence", and the like to be constructed by social and political narratives, discourses and practices that are rooted in specific contexts and vary across time. Accordingly, political violence is not a universal, concrete, and immutable fact, and acts of violence are not extraordinary occurrences that are unrelated to other social and political, violent or non-violent activities. Political violence is a "narrativistic" social reality, whose holistic nature informs both agent and observer according to their contextual and temporal dimensions (Spector-Mersel, 2010, p. 211).

In epistemological terms, I approach political violence through constructionism, conceiving it as a social phenomenon rather than an objective reality (Turk, 2004). This is aligned with CTS (see Jackson et al., 2011) and with the narrative paradigm (see Sparkes and Smith, 2008; Spector-Mersel, 2010; Esin, Fathi and Squire, 2013). Both standpoints highlight the fact that knowledge production is a social process that is always tied to a particular context, in which a story is not only co-constructed between interviewer and interviewee but also influenced by broader social, interpersonal, cultural, and power relations. In this vein, in this book, I explore how, through fieldwork, I came into direct contact with the real people behind academic assumptions, established personal relationships with them, and strove to grasp the complexity of their lives in order to represent their perspectives in an accurate manner and enrich our knowledge of political violence. Thereby, the individuals I met in the field became research partners rather than cold objects of study. I co-constructed meanings with them and reconstructed their lived experiences. Such a constructionist epistemology is based on a

> socio-cultural-oriented approach that conceptualises human beings as meaning-makers who use narratives to interpret, direct and communicate life and to configure and constitute their experience and their sense of who they are. These narratives are passed down from people's social and cultural world.
>
> (Smith, 2016, p. 204)

However, narratives can never be taken as ultimate products, because their dialogical nature involves elements that are liable to change over time, affecting the tellers' perspectives and positioning in the narrative process. In addition, in this book, I assign relevance to contextual variables, including interpersonal and gender dynamics. I acknowledge that the nature of the research process has different ideological, political, and ethical layers. Moreover, I argue that there is no ultimate truth about political violence. Yet, when scholarly standards and procedures are applied, some relatively secure knowledge claims may be made, whilst always recognising and reflecting on the researcher's influence on the research project and on the social, political, and contextual factors that frame it. Ultimately, this book is epistemologically committed to supporting the assertion that "the point of knowledge is not just to understand the world, but to change it for the better" (Jackson et al., 2011, p. 31).

Data collection through interviews involves close personal interactions and the generation of potentially powerful knowledge. This implies adherence to high ethical standards throughout the research process, particularly when it covers sensitive topics, such as politically motivated violence. During interviews, the researcher acts as both participant and observer; yet, not all interviewees are aware of this double role. This is especially true when the researcher presents herself as very interested in the subject, friendly, and trustworthy (with the latter supported by information sheets, consent forms, and impressive university credentials). In this context, responsibility for the collected data lies with the researcher, who must reflect on the potential "societal uses of the knowledge produced by academic social science interviews" (Kvale, 2006, p. 497). Particular attention must also be paid to the possible personal, social, and political impact of the research on its participants and the ways they should be ethically protected. Therefore, ethical concerns should not be limited to certain stages of the research (e.g., data collection) or to certain people (e.g., only the interviewees). Rather, they should be considered throughout the process – from the moment when potential interviewees are asked to participate in the study to analysis and final presentation of their accounts – and in relation to all of the parties involved (researcher, interviewees, readers, thesis supervisor and so on).

Hence, in my fieldwork, each interviewee was briefed at the start of their interview about the aims of the study and they always received a final verbatim transcript of the interview. This gave them an opportunity to correct any inaccuracies, ensure that their views were correctly represented, and cut any sections that made them feel uncomfortable. At this stage, I again requested informed consent from the interviewees, as suggested by Ruthellen Josselson (2007), in order to clarify that I, as a researcher, planned to use their statements to shed light on the subject under analysis, not to publicise their private lives. In addition, I clarified that their stories would be treated as possible versions of the social world so that they would not feel betrayed or expect me to affirm or endorse their version of events (see Dingwall, 1980). Finally, I anonymised all of the transcripts and carefully selected the most illuminating extracts in order to protect the interviewees' identities and produce a coherent and detailed account of their experiences.

This concern with anonymity and confidentiality, even when interviewees insist that their names may be used, is justified on the grounds that the greatest risk in ethnography occurs once the work is published, because at that stage it may be used or interpreted in ways that the researcher cannot control. I became acutely conscious of this issue when one interviewee explained what had happened after her story was published in a book the previous year. Her eleven-year-old grandson had asked her whether she had "been like those people who fly planes at skyscrapers". Although this interviewee's organisation had never threatened human lives, this proved to be a particularly difficult and disturbing question, because she did not know how to explain her activities to such a young person. Consequently, she told her grandson that she would return to the subject when he was old enough to understand. Clearly, then, as Elizabeth Murphy and Robert Dingwall (2002, p. 342) assert, "the publication of ethnographic accounts may expose individuals to other versions of reality held by those close to them, breaking down protective silences". Hence, anonymity and confidentiality should be maintained not only to ensure the ethical protection of interviewees but also to balance the inevitable power relations between researcher and researched. Such relations are often perceived as oppressive and exploitative by feminist and post-colonial researchers. They consider that truly ethical research is impossible (see, e.g., Patai, 1991), and that attempting to interpret others' experiences is "a new form of colonisation" (Murphy and Dingwall, 2002, p. 345). However, other authors argue that power relations do not necessarily lead to exploitation, and that the latter results only when researchers achieve their objectives at real cost to their participants (Wolf, 1996). From my perspective, I feel that researchers must give interviewees ample opportunity to edit their final transcripts, and they must relate the interviewees' stories in a way that respects their origins and intentions, while at the same time presenting their own analysis of the issue under discussion.

Finally, I agree with Kum-Kum Bhavnani (1990, p. 141) that "the assumption that empowerment is necessarily synonymous with 'giving a voice' is not a valid one", because bringing silenced voices to the fore can be disempowering through the reproduction of social stereotypes. Thus, it is of vital importance to understand the political, economic and social framework that allows certain voices to be silenced, but also to be clear regarding who is being empowered through the research process. With respect to the latter point, and in line with Bhavnani (1990, p. 149), the researcher should aim to give interviewees a voice that will "begin to present narratives: and that through their narratives, people may be moved beyond their words to the possibility of action. That is, that they may begin to realise their capacity to create history".

Political narratives, identity and the Dialogical Self Theory

Since the "narrative turn" in the social sciences, cultural studies, and psychology, which started in the 1980s, narrative has been seen not only as material that may be collected for analysis, but also as a method and a lens in itself. Underlying this turn is, among other aspects, the "life as narrative" metaphorical lens, which advocates that narratives have a particular role in the study of human lives (Polkinghorne, 1988; Bruner, 1991; McAdams, 1993). Although the narrative turn has brought considerable scholarly attention to the connection between narratives and identity, this connection remains "more asserted than demonstrated" (Polletta, Chen, Gardner and Motes, 2011, p. 113) due to the scarcity of empirical studies. Moreover, more recently, there has been growing interest in studying the relationship between narrative and politics, which has generated the expression "political narratives" (see, e.g., Davis, 2002; Polletta, 2006; Andrews, 2007; Zingaro, 2009; Selbin, 2010). However, little is still known regarding political narratives' underlying engagement with, life within, and disengagement from an armed organisation at the micro-level. In other words, we have heard few stories told by former militants about their experiences of politically motivated violence. As a result, this book contributes to a better understanding of the link between political narratives and identity, and the processes underlying engagement with, life within, and disengagement from an armed organisation more generally.

To explore this, I pay attention to micro-level political narratives. These are the stories former militants tell about "how the world works, how they explain the engines of social change, and the role they see themselves, and those whom they regard as being part of their group" (Andrews, 2007, p. 8). I will also take into account macro-level political narratives. These are larger clusters of national and international stories in which individuals position themselves (Andrews, 2014). The latter represent the contextual "cultural stock of plots" (Polletta, 2006, p. 10) or the "cultural narratives" (Rice, 2002, p. 82) that give primacy to certain stories to the detriment of others. Such macro-level political narratives portray the remembered and the forgotten stories. They can be found, for instance, in history textbooks or in public officials' speeches at key national events. In this context, the stories former militants tell about their lives and the socio-political culture of their society constitute the building blocks of individual identity, informing how the self and others are perceived. Such stories may be found at the origin of the possibility or impossibility of change.

To analyse the link between political narratives and identity, this book will employ the DST. According to Hubert Hermans (1996), this theoretical perspective sees the self as plural, dynamic, and multivocal. Thus, individuals may inhabit different positions in the dialogical space of their selves, voicing in singular and distinctive ways a particular experience. Individuals give meaning to life's experiences and events through these continuous dialogues, real or imagined, which happen within the self-system. For instance, the accounts of former militants that appear in this book showcase not only the *I as a militant* or *I as a former militant* identity positions, but also the *I as a mother* or *I as a student* identity positions. In this context, through the agentic powers of the "I", each individual may "imaginatively endow each position with a voice" (Hermans, 2002, p. 148). Such imaginative endowment results in the composite I-positions, which portray both the continuity and the discontinuity that occur in the dialogical self (Hermans and Kempen, 1993). On the one hand, continuity is provided by the "I" itself, since "it is *one and the same I* who is doing this" (Hermans and Hermans-Konopka, 2010, p. 139; original emphasis). On the other hand, discontinuity is connected to the opposing positions sheltered by the self that threaten its stability. For some former militants in this book, at certain moments in time, the positions *I as a committed militant* and *I as a mother* entered into conflict. One of them had to dominate the other to maintain the stability of the identity system. This led Mariana, whose story appeared in the Introduction, to develop pro-disengagement I-positions when she became pregnant after spending six years under a clandestine identity in the FP-25. In order to adopt her *I as a mother* identity position, she had to subjugate her *I as a committed militant* identity position. Thus, the DST proposes that our phenomenological sense of unity is the result of the dialogue between different I-positions, as well as their dynamic movements in the dialogical space.

The I-positions can be both internal (the voices that are perceived as part of the individual) and external (the voices of others), present or absent, singular (e.g., "My grandfather" in Mariana's story) or generalised (e.g., "The military" in Afonso's story; also in the Introduction). Internal positions tend to be introduced with the personal pronoun "I" (e.g., "I as a militant"). External positions are felt as aspects of the environment, but their voices are assimilated and integrated in the self. They tend to be preceded by the possessive determiner "my" (e.g., "My comrade"). Significant others are not the only ones who have a space in the identity arena. Individuals' socio-cultural contexts – the collective voice (e.g., "My village's culture" in Gustavo's story; in Chapter 3) – do, too. It is among collective positions that we find the macro-level political narratives. They are external to individuals and can have an impact in the way they perceive themselves and the world by coming into dialogue and co-constructing meaning with individual positions (Hermans and Kempen, 1993; Hermans, 2001). In this vein, internal meanings are always created under the influence of the historical, social, cultural, and political contexts of a certain time and place. This is clearly demonstrated through the three stories in the Introduction, and it will be underlined in subsequent chapters.

As such, each narrative of the self, each perspective of others, each view of reality is the result of the temporary dominance of a set of I-positions that is not predefined but constantly recreated. Thereby, some I-positions may be temporarily silent, while others may form a coalition, and still others may oppose the dominant ones, leading to conflict and disrupting the temporary dominance of a specific set of positions. In this sense, behind each story that is told, there is a multivocal self in continuous dialogue. In this book, in each period of time in the life cycle of each former militant, it is possible to see this dance of positions. In the engagement phase, for instance, it is possible to discern both pro-engagement positions – *I as a militant who perceives violence as necessary* – and counter-engagement positions – *I as a father who will leave my children behind*. In most cases, as we shall see, family-related positions were subjugated in the engagement phase. However, they sometimes gained strength over time and ultimately became key pro-disengagement positions for members of politically violent organisations.

Difficulties in dealing with the dialogue among different I-positions (internal, external, collective) may lead individuals to silence alternative I-positions and seek refuge in a set of highly dominant positions. This was evident in some former militants' accounts of perpetuating the fight even though they knew they were at high risk of arrest or even death. However, the coalition of identity positions around the central *I as a committed militant*, including the likes of *I as a loyal comrade*, was too strong. In such cases, the alternative – pro-disengagement – I-positions were silenced and relegated to the periphery, while centripetal forces, working towards unity, dominated the self (Hermans, 2002). In this type of scenario, diversity, innovation, and dialogue are replaced by repetitive meanings and dominant narratives, giving way to monologue. This creates a dominant perspective of the self, others, and the world (Hermans, 1996). However, the dialogical nature of the self, even in deeply monologized circumstances, ensures the existence of counter-positions, even though they are silent and constrained.

Conversely, a dialogical form of interaction among the distinct I-positions allows their perspectives to be manifested. Although differences in power may be present, their more or less equal rights to contribute to the outcome of the interactions are assumed (Hermans and Hermans-Konopka, 2010). This dialogue among positions is usually expressed in the narrative's flexibility. When different voices are heard, the resulting narrative is more open and integrative of the different I-positions of the self. This leads to a more complex and adaptive construction of meaning. Views of the self, others, and the world tend to be more complex when the self leans to the dialogical side, and centrifugal forces, working towards differentiation, emerge in the self and create openness to change and innovation (Hermans, 2002). In Chapter 5, we see good examples of this dialogical form of dialogue among I-positions when former militants explain how they have reworked their pasts in their current selves. They had to find ways to maintain the continuity of their identity systems while justifying the discontinuities, such as leaving violence behind. It is true that some former militants, particularly those who feel that their goals have been achieved, consider that they have not changed one iota; rather, the context did. However, in most cases, former militants accept that they had to review and adapt their socio-political views because, over time, they gained, for example, a different historical awareness. Thus, today, their self is inhabited by their past position, but also by formerly silenced positions and new positions, which are continually reconstructed through the stories they tell about their lives.

In this book, I will also show that the conflict generated by opposing positions may be solved through two different processes: dominance reversal or negotiation (Hermans, 1996). When dominance reversal occurs, a formerly dominant position is now dominated, and the subjugated voice comes to the fore. The potential for change in dominance reversal is much lower than in negotiation, as it leans to the monological side. When negotiation occurs, the positions engage in dialogue and are quite open to change. Often, in the context of negotiation, it is possible to find specific I-positions functioning as mediators in the dialogue. These can be third positions, which act as mediators between conflicting positions. For instance, as explored in Chapter 4, before Artur's engagement with the ARA, he was divided between the positions *I as a student* and *I as someone who believes that armed action is needed to assist the overthrow of the dictatorship.* He could not maintain both positions because the latter meant going underground. In these circumstances, the context of political repression he was experiencing led Artur to bring forward a couple of third positions to help him make a choice: *I as a martyr–hero* and *I as one of the few people who is prepared to fight the regime.* These third positions did not solve the conflict within Artur's self. He still regretted his inability to finish his studies. Yet, they helped him to make a pro-engagement decision by subjugating a counter-engagement position (*I as a student*).

Another type of position that is found in the context of negotiation is the meta-position. The development of such a position allows the articulation of two or more previously conflicting positions, but also the creation of new meanings. Meta-positions play an extremely important role in change (see, e.g., Leiman and Stiles, 2001; Cooper, 2003; Hermans, 2003; Hermans and Hermans-Jansen, 2004; Hermans and Hermans-Konopka, 2010). By creating distance from the other I-positions, meta-positions achieve a comprehensive view. They can be imagined as mediators between opposed or different positions, alleviating conflict. Through meta-positions, the different stories that emerge from a multivocal self may be integrated into a complex, dynamic, and coherent narrative script (Hermans, 2006). In this book, meta-positions can be found both at the origin of pro-engagement and pro-disengagement positions. For instance, today, some former militants deal with the diversity of past, present, and future positions within their selves through the meta-position *I as a reflective former militant*. This meta-position allows them to acknowledge their past choices and experiences, but also to come to terms with the fact that they are no longer committed militants. It is not as if they do not care about socio-political issues any more, or as if they simply agree with how such issues have evolved, or how they have been addressed. It is just that their reflections on their past militancy and on everything that happened thereafter no longer lead them to advocate politically motivated violence. They pursue, instead, other forms of activism.

Data: co-creating and analysing stories

Personal stories of involvement in politically motivated violence are the focus of this book. These stories have been little explored in the Portuguese context and, as José Pacheco Pereira (2013) notes, they can be retrieved only from the memories of former militants. However, I believe that personal stories are socially constructed and cannot be taken as representations of *the* reality; rather, they are representations of *a* reality. Stories are the vehicles through which individuals represent their experiences, based on the narratives that are available to them in their temporal and spatial locations. Thus, story and narrative are different. As Brett Smith (2016) argues, "people tell stories, not narratives". Stories draw on their cultural knowledge, on their relationship with the receiver, and on the shared and divergent understandings of stories in different contexts (Gubrium and Holstein, 1997).

In this vein, this book comprises what Toros (2008, p. 289) has called "experiential data". Such data was collected in 2013 through in-depth interviews with twenty-eight former Portuguese militants who had been members of a total of six organisations. This data collection was actually a process of data co-construction. It is true that I returned home with palpable data, but it is not as if I had no influence whatsoever in the course of its collection. That would be impossible. My influence on the process began with the way in which I was perceived by most of the interviewees – as a stranger who was working towards her doctorate. Although there were variations in the reactions of the interviewees, our conversations were generally characterised by a patronising tone, based on the assumption that I did not share their lived experiences in terms of socio-political context and reality. While some adopted what I would describe as a grandparent-patronising tone, others adopted more of an offensive-patronising tone. The former observed their duties as storytellers, as guardians of past realities that needed to be communicated to a member of a younger generation who had not lived through such harsh times and consequently needed quite a lot of detail if she were to understand what was being recounted. The latter assumed that I was too young to possess sufficient knowledge to complete the task I had set myself, which resulted in one interviewee addressing me as "baby", two describing me as "the little doctor", and another repeatedly informing me that my project was "rubbish".

The interviewees also tended to ask personal questions throughout the interview process. In most cases, they simply wanted to trace the origins of my research interests, asking questions about my academic path. However, some of them wanted to know more about my family and where I grew up. One asked how many children I was planning to have and if my husband treated me well. At the end of the interview, he offered a piece of advice, because he was very impressed by the fact that my husband waited in the car during our three-hour conversation. He told me to treat him well and not to abuse his patience. At the time, despite answering honestly – which was the least I could do, given that I was asking people who had never met me before to share sensitive information – I found his questions and advice quite odd and rather too detailed. Yet, for him, they made total sense, as I came to understand later, when reflecting on the interview. Family was always at the heart of his stories.

I also stumbled on a group of interviewees, all from the same organisation, who tried to steer the research in a particular direction by allowing access only to former comrades whom they knew would reiterate their viewpoints. I do not mean to imply that these were the only interviewees who attempted to do this. However, they were much more determined than the others, strongly discouraging me from talking to anyone outside of the small circle of people they had selected for interview.

Thus, the interaction point when stories were co-created, as well as other points of contact throughout the research process (e.g., when I asked interviewees if they wished to revise their transcripts), contributed to how those stories were analysed. This meant that the story of how the stories were collected had to be taken into account. This story left me, initially, feeling antagonistic about some stories and passionate about others. All stories have the power to do this. They act in people's lives and set courses of action. However, I was aware of this and determined to fight what Antonius Robben (1995, p. 83) has called "ethnographic seduction", which happens when the researcher sides with certain interviewees' stories unreservedly, leading to an absence of any critical insight. In my case, I found myself siding excitingly with some stories and devaluing others. Therefore, I examined my own life story for possible inhibitions, weaknesses, and biases. Obviously, I found several. For instance, I am a strong supporter of the April Revolution. I grew up celebrating it, even though I was born more than ten years after it had happened. Consequently, it was predictable that my favourite stories were not about countering that revolution. In this vein, I had to be rigorous in distinguishing between empathy and seduction in order to retain the same level of interest and understanding regarding all of the stories, because they are all equally valuable to accomplish this book's goal of offering detailed descriptions of political violence in various moments of time and different socio-political circumstances.

Therefore, my analysis of the stories forced me to grapple with the stances of objectivity, neutrality, and detachment that are so often reified by academic convention. All stories – and particularly life stories – carry emotions and cause emotional responses in the listener. However, scholarly research often ignores the emotions that the researcher feels during the research process and chooses to present the researcher as an entirely objective scientific observer, rather than a subjective humanistic participant. Nevertheless, I found that the emotions triggered at various stages of my research were actually valuable, just as other scholars have (e.g., Kleinman and Copp, 1993; Holstein and Gubrium, 2004). Sometimes, they helped me to empathise with life experiences I have never had. At other times, they forced me to stop and recalibrate preconceived ideas not only to avoid favouritism but also to deal with difficult stories. Some of the interviewees' stories, particularly those concerning assassinations, made me feel nauseous and sad. Fortunately, this reaction never had a significant impact on the conversation. It was not that I stopped listening when they talked about such issues; rather, inside my head, I was busy multi-tasking. I listened to what they had to say, tried to make sense of it in relation to the question I had asked, formulated a follow-up question that would elicit further information, maintained eye-contact, and so on. The strong emotions came later, usually in the stillness of the night. I found it very confusing the first time it happened. I felt like crying, tried to stop thinking about it, and attempted to distance myself from it all. However, when it continued to happen and I read about other researchers' experiences (e.g., Andrews, 1991; Riessman, 2005; Hydén, 2013; Daigle, 2016), I started my own embodiment of such stories. I started to notice that my body reacted to different stories in different ways and gained an understanding of what these reactions meant. For instance, when my stomach cramped, I knew that a story was making me feel particularly uncomfortable, so I would make an extra effort to engage with it. This helped me to live with the stories, even the very difficult ones, and to increase my understanding of the individuals behind them, which in turn enabled me to represent their politically violent militancy accurately, if only partially.

Moreover, when analysing former militants' accounts, I had to bear in mind that the telling of life stories is intimately connected to memory dynamics. This is because, as Paul Ricoeur (1981, p. 176) has pointed out, despite our perception of "the story" as a whole that is continually unfolding, we are, in effect, "reading the end in the beginning and the beginning in the end". However, this does not happen in isolation, "but in intimate interaction with a complex set (or setting) of larger stories still" (Randall, 2010, p. 151), because stories are "in part profound societal memory, meaning and message" (Selbin, 2010, p. 28). In other words, stories make sense of events embedded in the collective memory but also contribute to the establishment of institutional facts as a shared past, forming the basis for the narration of new events. Thus, "memory is not simply a private affair" (Randall, 2010, p. 156) and, by its very nature, it misrepresents the past. As William Randall

(2010, p. 160) asserts: "Romanticizing, fantasizing, embellishing, embroidering, shrinking, stretching: all of these, to some degree, are inevitable – and normal – whenever we remember. We can never succeed in recalling things exactly as they happened". This was exactly what one of my interviewees, Henrique from the LUAR, tried to tell me. The role of narrator of the past made him feel uncomfortable. In recounting his story, he feared a lack of authenticity because he was aware that he was "dealing with a memory, not the reality of that time".

This fluidity of memory has been linked to wider debates within the social sciences regarding conceptions and assumptions of truth, which usually refer to what actually happened (see Miller, 2000). However, as already mentioned, where memory is concerned, this objective truth is unobtainable. Nevertheless, a different conception of truth is proposed by different scholars who focus, for instance, on "textual truth" (Freeman, 2003, 2010) or "social truth" (Selbin, 2010, p. 32). These types of truths represent "a performance of memory talk serving particular personal and social functions through the stories that are told to explain who we are, what we are, and where we are in life at a particular time and place" (Randall and Phoenix, 2009, p. 127). Additionally, the act of storytelling is selective because, "[u]p to a point, it is possible to tell several stories based on the same events" through their organisation around different plots (Ricoeur, 1996, p. 6). Thus, stories reconfigure "our confused, unformed, and at the limit mute temporal experience" (Ricoeur, 1984, p. xi). Consequently, when analysing former militants' stories, I kept in mind that each individual does not have a life story, but many stories, which do not inevitably amalgamate into an overall coherent storyline. Thus, each individual can become whatever story they want to be.

Thereby, in this book, I cannot subscribe the naive realist view of qualitative research where the researcher simply "gives voice" to the participants (see Fine, 2002). Over the whole research process, I can see my fingerprints on numerous theoretical, paradigmatic and methodological choices. However, these fingerprints were left behind as a result of informed and carefully considered choices, not as a result of bias, partisanship, or subjectivity, which, according to Sluka (1989), are likely accusations when one chooses to study highly political and controversial subjects. In light of these reflections, I committed myself to representing a (possible) voice in relation to each interviewee's story, and to examining my personal influence on the research process from beginning to end.

Conclusion

This chapter has outlined the conceptual and theoretical underpinnings of the analysis presented in the following three chapters. Through the Dialogical Self Theory, described in this chapter, I will identify the existing identity positions throughout three specific moments in the life of a former militant: engagement with, life within, and disengagement from a politically violent organisation.

This exercise will shed light on both personal and contextual factors at the origin of the identity positions that led individuals to engage with armed organisations, and on how such identity positions can go through change processes, leading some individuals to abandon violence. In Chapter 3, I begin by exploring the origins of the personal political awareness that facilitated the development of pro-engagement identity positions.

References

Andrews, M. (1991) *Lifetimes of commitment*. Cambridge: Cambridge University Press.

Andrews, M. (2007) *Shaping history: narratives of political change*. Cambridge: Cambridge University Press.

Andrews, M. (2014) 'Narrating moments of political change', in Capelos, T., Kinnvall, C. and Nesbitt-Larking, P. W. (eds) *The Palgrave handbook of global political psychology*. New York: Palgrave Macmillan, pp. 353–368.

Bhavnani, K. K. (1990) 'What's power got to do with it? Empowerment and social research', in Parker, I. and Shotter, J. (eds) *Deconstructing social psychology*. London: Routledge, pp. 141–152.

Bruner, J. (1991) 'The narrative construction of reality', *Critical Inquiry*, 18(1), p. 1.

Cooper, M. (2003) '"I-I" and "I-me": rransposing Buber's interpersonal attitudes to the intrapersonal plane', *Journal of Constructivist Psychology*, 16(2), pp. 131–153.

Cox, R. W. (1986) 'Social forces, states, and world orders: beyond international relations theory', in Keohane, R. O. (ed.) *Neorealism and its critics*. New York: Columbia University Press, pp. 204–254.

Daigle, M. (2016) 'Writing the lives of others: storytelling and international politics', *Millennium: Journal of International Studies*, 45(1), pp. 25–42.

Davis, J. (2002) 'Narrative and social movements: the power of stories', in Davis, J. (ed.) *Stories of change: narrative and social movements*. Albany, NY: SUNY Press, pp. 3–29.

Dingwall, R. (1980) 'Ethics and ethnography', *Sociological Review*, 28, pp. 871–891.

Esin, C., Fathi, M. and Squire, C. (2013) 'Narrative analysis: the constructionist approach', in Flick, U. (ed.) *The Sage handbook of qualitative data analysis*. London: Sage, pp. 203–216.

Fine, M. (2002) *Disruptive voices: the possibilities for feminist research*. Ann Arbor: University of Michigan Press.

Freeman, M. (2003) 'Rethinking the fictive, reclaiming the real: autobiography, narrative time, and the burden of truth', in Fireman, G., McVay, T. and Flanagan, O. (eds) *Narrative and consciousness: literature, psychology, and the brain*. New York: Oxford University Press, pp. 115–128.

Freeman, M. (2010) *Hindsight: the promise and peril of looking backward*. New York: Oxford University Press.

Gubrium, J. F. and Holstein, J. A. (1997) *The new language of qualitative method*. New York andOxford: Oxford University Press.

Gunning, J. (2007) 'A case for Critical Terrorism Studies?', *Government and Opposition*, 42(3), pp. 363–393.

Heath-Kelly, C. (2013) *Politics of violence: militancy, international politics, killing in the name*. London: Routledge.

Hermans, H. J. M. (1996) 'Voicing the self: from information processing to dialogical interchange', *Psychological Bulletin*, 119(1), pp. 31–50.

Hermans, H. J. M. (2001) 'The dialogical self: toward a theory', *Culture and Psychology*, 7(3), pp. 243–281.

Hermans, H. J. M. (2002) 'The dialogical self as a society of mind', *Theory and Psychology*, 12(2), pp. 147–160.

Hermans, H. J. M. (2003) 'The construction and reconstruction of a dialogical self', *Journal of Constructivist Psychology*, 16(2), pp. 89–130.

Hermans, H. J. M. (2006) 'The self as a theatre of voices: disorganization and reorganization of a position repertoire', *Journal of Constructivist Psychology*, 19(2), pp. 147–169.

Hermans, H. J. M. and Hermans-Jansen, E. (2004) 'The dialogical construction of coalitions in a personal position repertoire', in *The dialogical self in psychotherapy*. New York: Brunner-Routledge, pp. 124–137.

Hermans, H. J. M. and Hermans-Konopka, A. (2010) *Dialogical Self Theory: positioning and counter-positioning in a globalizing society*. Cambridge: Cambridge University Press.

Hermans, H. J. M. and Kempen, H. (1993) *Dialogical self: meaning as movements*. San Diego, CA: Academic Press.

Hoffman, M. (1987) 'Critical theory and the inter-paradigm debate', *Millennium: Journal of International Studies*, 17(1), pp. 91–95.

Holstein, J. A. and Gubrium, J. F. (2004) 'Context: working it up, down, and across', in Seale, C., Gobo, G., Gubrium, J. F. and Silverman, D. (eds) *Qualitative research practice*. London: Sage, pp. 267–281.

Horkheimer, M. (1992) *Eclipse of reason*. New York: Continuum.

Hydén, L.-C. (2013) 'Bodies, embodiment and stories', in Andrews, M., Squire, C. and Tamboukou, M. (eds) *Doing narrative research*. 2nd Edition. London: Sage, pp. 126–141.

Jackson, R. (2007) 'Introduction: the case for Critical Terrorism Studies', *European Political Science*, 6(3), pp. 225–227.

Jackson, R. (2008) 'An argument for terrorism', *Perspectives on Terrorism*, 2(2), pp. 25–32.

Jackson, R. (2015) 'Towards critical peace research: lessons from Critical Terrorism Studies', in Tellidis, I. and Toros, H. (eds) *Researching terrorism, peace and conflict studies: interaction, synthesis and opposition*. London: Routledge, pp. 19–37.

Jackson, R., Jarvis, L., Gunning, J. and Smyth, M. (2011) *Terrorism: a critical introduction*. Basingstoke: Palgrave Macmillan.

Josselson, R. (2007) 'The ethical attitude in narrative research: principles and practicalities', in Clandinin, D. J. (ed.) *Handbook of narrative inquiry*. Thousand Oaks, CA: Sage, pp. 537–566.

Kleinman, S. and Copp, M. (1993) *Emotions and fieldwork*. London: Sage.

Kvale, S. (2006) 'Dominance through interviews and dialogues', *Qualitative Inquiry*, 12 (3), pp. 480–500.

Leiman, M. and Stiles, W. B. (2001) 'Dialogical sequence analysis and the zone of proximal development as conceptual enhancements to the assimilation model: the case of Jan revisited', *Psychotherapy Research*, 11(3), pp. 311–330.

Mahmood, C. (1996) *Fighting for faith and nation: dialogues with Sikh militants*. Philadelphia: University of Pennsylvania Press.

McAdams, D. P. (1993) *The stories we live by: personal myths and the making of the self.* New York: William Morrow.

Miller, R. (2000) *Researching life stories and family histories.* London: Sage.

Morgan, G. and Smircich, L. (1980) 'The case for qualitative research', *Academy of Management Review*, 5(4), pp. 491–500.

Murphy, E. and Dingwall, R. (2002) 'The ethics of ethnography', in Atkinson, P., Coffey, A., Delamont, S., Lofland, J. and Lofland, L. (eds) *Handbook of ethnography.* London: Sage, pp. 339–351.

Patai, D. (1991) 'US academics and Third World women: is ethical research possible?', in Gluck, S. and Patai, D. (eds) *Women's words: the feminist practice of oral history.* New York: Routledge, pp. 137–153.

Pereira, J. P. (2013) *As armas de papel: publicações periódicas clandestinas e do exílio ligadas a movimentos radicais de esquerda cultural e política (1963–1974).* Lisbon: Temas e Debates – Círculo de Leitores.

Polkinghorne, D. (1988) *Narrative knowing and the human sciences.* New York: SUNY Press.

Polletta, F. (2006) *It was like a fever: storytelling in protest and politics.* Chicago: University of Chicago Press.

Polletta, F., Chen, P., Gardner, B. and Motes, A. (2011) 'The sociology of storytelling', *Annual Review of Sociology*, 31(1), pp. 109–130.

Randall, W. L. (2010) 'The narrative complexity of our past: in praise of memory's sins', *Theory and Psychology*, 20(2), pp. 147–169.

Randall, W. L. and Phoenix, C. (2009) 'The problem with truth in qualitative interviews: reflections from a narrative perspective', *Qualitative Research in Sport and Exercise*, 1(2), pp. 125–140.

Rice, J. S. (2002) 'Getting our stories straight: culture, narrative, and identity in the self-help movement', in Davis, J. (ed.) *Stories of change: narrative and social movements.* Albany, NY: SUNY Press, pp. 79–99.

Ricoeur, P. (1981) *Hermeneutics and the human sciences: essays on language, action and interpretation.* Cambridge: Cambridge University Press.

Ricoeur, P. (1984) *Time and narrative, Volume I.* Chicago: University of Chicago Press.

Ricoeur, P. (1996) 'Reflections on a new ethos for Europe', in Kearney, R. O. (ed.) *Paul Ricoeur: the hermeneutics of action.* London: Sage, pp. 3–13.

Riessman, C. K. (2005) 'Exporting ethics: a narrative about narrative research in South India', *Health: An Interdisciplinary Journal for the Social Study of Health, Illness and Medicine*, 9(4), pp. 473–490.

Robben, A. (1995) 'The politics of truth and emotion among victims and perpetrators of violence', in Nordstrom, C. and Robben, A. (eds) *Fieldwork under fire: contemporary studies of violence and survival.* Oakland, CA: University of California Press, pp. 81–103.

Sarbin, T. R. (1986) 'The narrative as root metaphor for psychology', in Sarbin, T. R. (ed.) *Narrative psychology: the storied nature of human conduct.* New York: Praeger, pp. 3–21.

Selbin, E. (2010) *Revolution, rebellion, resistance: the power of story.* London: Zed Books.

Sluka, J. (1989) *Hearts and minds, water and fish: support for the IRA and INLA in a Northern Irish ghetto.* Greenwich, CT: JAI Press.

Sluka, J. (2009) 'The contribution of anthropology to Critical Terrorism Studies', in Jackson, R., Breen-Smyth, M. and Gunning, J. (eds) *Critical Terrorism Studies: a new research agenda.* London: Routledge, pp. 138–155.

Smith, B. (2016) 'Narrative analysis', in Lyons, E. and Coyle, A. (eds) *Analysing qualitative data in psychology.* 2nd Edition. London: Sage, pp. 202–221.

Sparkes, A. and Smith, B. (2008) 'Narrative constructionist inquiry', in Holstein, J. and Gubrium, J. (eds) *Handbook of constructionist research.* London: Guilford Publications, pp. 295–314.

Spector-Mersel, G. (2010) 'Narrative research: time for a paradigm shift', *Narrative Inquiry*, 20(1), pp. 204–224.

Toros, H. (2008) 'Terrorists, scholars and ordinary people: confronting terrorism studies with field experiences', *Critical Studies on Terrorism*, 1(2), pp. 279–292.

Toros, H. (2012) *Terrorism, talking and transformation: a critical approach.* Abingdon: Routledge.

Toros, H. and Gunning, J. (2009) 'Exploring a critical theory approach to terrorism studies', in Jackson, R., Breen-Smyth, M. and Gunning, J. (eds) *Critical Terrorism Studies: a new research agenda.* London: Routledge, pp. 87–108.

Turk, A. T. (2004) 'Sociology of terrorism', *Annual Review of Sociology*, 30(1), pp. 271–286.

Wolf, M. (1996) 'Afterword: musing from an old grey wolf', in Wolf, D. (ed.) *Feminist dilemmas in fieldwork.* Oxford: Westview Press, pp. 215–221.

Zingaro, L. (2009) *Speaking out: storytelling for social change.* Walnut Creek, CA: Left Coast Press.

Zulaika, J. (1988) *Basque violence: metaphor and sacrament.* Reno: University of Nevada Press.

Zulaika, J. and Douglass, W. (1996) *Terror and taboo: the follies, fables and faces of terrorism.* London: Routledge.

3 Engagement with a politically violent organisation

> In the Alentejo, more than in the north, life was very hard for a lot of people. In the north, they also suffered a lot, but they had small properties, almost everyone had a little bit of land, and having a little bit of land is a support, you can go hungry, but you don't starve to death. In the Alentejo, people starved to death … We had the great big properties, which were thousands of hectares, and the poor had nothing, and what does that mean? It means people were in the hands of the landowners, so they had nothing … So, the people of the Alentejo suffered more, and it is no accident that they were more politically aware. It is not because we were smarter or dumber; it's because they suffered more. They earned next to nothing and accepted whatever they could get; they worked as slaves for fear of losing their jobs. This all began to create in us a certain political conscience.
>
> (Xavier from the ARA)

The motivation to engage with a politically violent organisation combines both individual and contextual factors. Such factors impact individuals' perceptions of the external reality, feeding grievances, as the quote above illustrates, and, at times, intensifying demands for violent action. Therefore, engagement with a politically violent organisation tends to happen in times of socio-political turmoil, which can introduce and socialise ordinary individuals to violent actions and strategies (della Porta, 2013). However, it is important to note that engaging with a politically violent organisation is also a meaningful process for the actor. It is very close to their heart, involving positive and negative experiences, reasons to feel proud and frustrated, both at the time of engagement and for the rest of their life. This will be shown throughout this chapter and in the next two.

In this process of engagement, it is often possible to witness the development of a revolutionary positioning that implies the pursuit of political ends through violent means. This is commonly known as "radicalisation", although this term is highly contested, since, like the term "terrorism", it can be used as a label to pursue certain political agendas to the detriment of others. However, in this book, I propose to study radicalisation as a *process*, which can be useful to enhance our understanding of the different life journeys taken by individuals in the direction of committing themselves to politically violent organisations. Nevertheless, a few caveats are necessary regarding the study of the radicalisation process in general, and in this book in particular. First, engagement and radicalisation are not one and the same process, since there can be engagement without radicalisation and vice-versa (Taylor and Horgan, 2006). Second, it remains unproven that radicalised views lead to violent action or that the transformation of such views affects action (Bjørgo and Horgan, 2009). Third, it is important to note that while radicalised views may open a path to the commission of politically motivated violence, they are not criminal or harmful in themselves (Expert Group on Violent Radicalisation, 2008). Fourth, the term "radicalisation" was rarely used by my interviewees. In fact, it was explicitly used only once – to describe an increase and intensification of political views in support of violence. However, various interviewees described what was, in effect, a radicalisation process when using words and expressions such as "I was politicised" and "my political awareness". These comments were connected to an abstract ideological dimension (e.g., being Marxist–Leninist or right-wing), but also to an awareness of social and political issues that led to a sense that a certain goal had to be pursued through violent means.

Thus, I propose studying the radicalisation process through the analysis of identity positions in former militants' life story narratives. I argue that understanding the intersection of social, political, historical, and personal circumstances through narrative identity can shed light on how and why certain events take place, and why individuals behave in certain ways. Life stories are rooted in the place, and time in which they exist and in the social relationships in which they are created, repeated, and transformed (Frank, 2010). They are shaped by the narrative resources available to individuals, which enable them to build relationships, establishing "cognitive and affective processes" that may gradually lead to violence and are strengthened by violence itself (della Porta, 2013, p. 19). Then, resorting to political violence is not automatic; rather, it is a process – "actions of some kind associated with other actions and reactions, often expressed in some sort of reciprocal relationship" (Taylor and Horgan, 2012, p. 130).

Therefore, in this chapter, I explore the seeds of engagement with politically violent organisations in the lives of former Portuguese militants. How and where were these seeds sown? How did different individuals – from different walks of life and with diverse political ideologies – take the step of committing to a politically violent organisation? In this vein, I start tracing the life stories of individuals who chose to engage in politically violent organisations in the past in Portugal. I shed light on the processes through which voice was given to certain internal and external, individual and collective I-positions, while ignoring or subjugating others. In this sense, I first outline the repertoire of political narratives at the outset of individual political awareness, which tells the story of how different ideological stances were cemented in individuals' lives through different socialisation agents. Second, I discuss the dynamics of commitment to a politically violent organisation, including the justifications for armed struggle. In both sections, I trace how former militants organise their selves through processes of meaning construction while attempting to understand themselves and describe themselves to an audience.

The origins of individual political awareness

My exploration of the origins of political awareness at the individual level emerged from the inevitable journeys interviewees made through their lives prior to committing to a politically violent organisation. In recounting those journeys, former militants aimed to explain who they were and where they came from. These accounts included personal details – regarding their family, for instance – as well as historical information regarding the spatial and temporal locations that influenced their decision to choose politically violent militancy. This last aspect had particular relevance because of the age difference between my interviewees and myself. In different moments, I sensed that they were concerned with providing complete accounts of their life stories, including various historical details. I believe that this was related to the way I was perceived. First, they knew that I had not shared their historical past. Second, I was seen as a representative of a broader audience – posterity. Thus, various interviewees located their stories in the experiential context of a particular generation, as if by understanding their generation I would understand how their political awareness and subsequent action developed.

Throughout this section, it is evident that different interviewees, in different moments of time, developed a consciousness of their location in the historical processes, which shaped their political awareness and framed their subsequent activities. Thus, this section includes my analysis of the individual stories of two generations of violent political activists in Portugal. The first of these generations may be characterised as "children of the regime", whose discourses, identities, and actions were shaped by the way they perceived and related to the *Estado Novo* regime. It encompasses two distinct types of militants: pre-revolution militants, who fought against *Estado Novo* from the 1960s until the April Revolution; and counter-revolution militants, who fought against the changes initiated by the April Revolution. The second generation may be characterised as "children of the revolution". It comprises post-revolution militants who were socialised and politicised in the euphoria of the April Revolution at a young age. They committed themselves to an armed organisation in the 1980s in a bid to realise the socialist promises of the revolution.

Pre-revolution militants: family and place of birth

Each of the pre-revolution militant interviewees mentioned the importance of their family in the development of their personal political awareness. Some also mentioned the significance of their birthplace. Various interviewees considered that their families, at an early stage, either explicitly or implicitly, cemented the political values for which they would fight in the future. In some cases, the tales of relatives who fought against the regime were extremely inspiring. For instance, Emílio from the LUAR talked about a "tradition of resistance" in his family, personified by a cousin who was arrested and sent to the Tarrafal forced labour camp. This voice of family resistance gave origin to the I-position *My family as traditionally part of the resistance*, which Emílio viewed as stronger and more influential than all of the extensive reading he had done on political matters. In the same vein, Gustavo, also from the LUAR, referred to his grandfather's republican activity during the monarchy, which had seen him imprisoned but had also inspired Gustavo's father's and his own convictions against the *Estado Novo*. Yet, in the case of these militants who acted during the dictatorship, such family influence was often implicit, because any overt political activity against the regime could be severely punished. Thus, parents would be very cautious, fearing not only for themselves but also for what might happen to their children if they engaged in oppositional politics. Nevertheless, many interviewees recognised the important role played by relatives who had discreetly countered the dominant narratives of the regime by exposing the younger generation to the social reality of the time. An example of this may be found in the story told by another former member of the LUAR, Diogo:

> I'm from a time when teachers at school would always make great speeches: "Now, with Salazar, there are no more poor people, the roads are good, the houses are good, the people are happy" and so on. Then I used to go home and tell all of that to my father, and he never once said it wasn't true. Never! We lived with great hardship, but on Sundays, we would always go for a wander around an area near where we lived. My father would always find a way of showing me the homes of extremely poor people. I do not know how people lived in such appalling conditions. The roads were full of potholes, the state of the schools and so on – that opened my eyes. He never actually said what we were told was wrong, because otherwise I might go and tell the teacher, "My dad says that's not true!" So, he did his political work in this way. I think it had a great impact on me.

Diogo's story showcases some of the political narratives of the regime that I explored in Chapter 1, such as *Salazar as the saviour of the nation* and *Salazar as the ruler who restored the country's finances*. Such a portrayal was spread through various channels at the regime's disposal, including the education system. However, the image painted by the regime's propaganda did not correspond to reality as Diogo's father knew all too well, and as he subtly revealed to his son during their Sunday excursions. Later in life, Diogo reached the conclusion that this was his father's form of political action and that it made a lasting contribution to his own political awareness.

Places of origin were also very important sources of external influence on young individuals' perceptions of the political world. Gustavo from the LUAR, for instance, described how the strong anti-regime positions that were prevalent within his village influenced his personal position of *I as naively socialised into anti-Estado Novo views from an early age*. For a couple of other pre-revolution militants, during the dictatorship, the *I come from the Alentejo* position conveyed a high probability of being against the regime. The Alentejo is a large region in the south of Portugal, between Lisbon and the Algarve, geographically marked by its extensive rolling plains. Its population had traditionally relied on agriculture, livestock rearing, and forestry. However, according to Xavier from the ARA, during the *Estado Novo*, these sectors were in the hands of a few landowners who would pay their workers very low wages and offer little in the way of job security. This created a context of extreme poverty and injustice that strengthened political opposition in the Alentejo, attracting the attention of the clandestine PCP. As Rita, also from the ARA, affirmed: "that area provided many members for the party [PCP], which was only natural because it was the only force that brought some hope to the people. People had nothing to lose, really". Subsequently, coming from the Alentejo meant coming from an area marked by resistance to the regime, a place where daily hardship made people acutely aware of the need to fight against the system and for justice. In this sense, people from the Alentejo were more likely to join the ranks of the PCP, which was the only active opposition party in the country during the *Estado Novo*, even though it was prohibited by the regime and hence obliged to stay underground, as noted in Chapter 1.

In the case of Rita, her parents went underground to work for the PCP, leaving her with her grandparents until she finished primary school. At the age of ten she went underground herself, mainly motivated by the strong position *I as a normal child who wants to live with her parents*: "I could not live with my grandparents for ever. I wanted to join my parents". Nowadays, Rita believes that external positions linked to being raised to see the misery and repression in which people lived contributed equally to strengthening her desire to join her parents not only as a daughter but also as a militant. This can be seen through the position *I did what had to be done*, or, in Rita's own words: "It was the natural thing to do". This is a core position of Rita's identity system. She uses it as a lens to look at her past militancy and justify her choices, which at times involved great sacrifice. She described, for instance, the limitations of life underground: "We could not go to the movies, we could not play, we could not have close friendships, we could not have a boyfriend. Everything was very limited, so people would not suspect us". She also explained that she questioned her choice during adolescence: "When we enter adolescence, we understand everything better. At that point, we can ask ourselves: 'Do I want to stay here or not?'" Her final decision was: "Continuity is usually the normal way". Over time, Rita's decision matured politically, leading her not only to remain underground but also to enrol in a training course in the Soviet Union when she turned eighteen. At that time, she met her future husband – the aforementioned Artur – with whom she resumed an underground life upon their return to Portugal, founding the armed organisation ARA. Again, this was something that Rita considered "normal", and in her opinion "well done", because "everything" was "working to overthrow the regime".

The repetition of the word "normal" throughout Rita's interview is interesting: it was "normal" for her to wish to join her clandestine parents; it was "normal" for her to remain underground; and it was "normal" for her to found an armed organisation to fight the regime. In fact, what Rita considered "normal" in her personal story represents choices she made that were motivated by the meanings she chose to give to her life. Such meanings crystallised into identity positions that encompassed three basic characteristics of her early life story:

1 The I-positions *I as a normal child who wants to live with her parents* and *I as the wife of the ARA's co-founder* are relational: Rita simply wanted to be reunited with her parents; and, later, her involvement with the ARA was closely related to the fact that she was the partner of one of the organisation's founders.
2 The I-position *I did what had to be done* is societal and historical: the need to fight an oppressive and violent regime despite great personal sacrifice strongly influenced Rita's socialisation.
3 These I-positions are not deterministic but set out a variety of possibilities for action: along the way, Rita had opportunities to turn in different directions, but she always chose "continuity".

Thus, Rita's choices, like those of every human being, were influenced by the different internal and external positions at work within herself, setting the course of her unique life story (Brockmeier, 2009).

Therefore, the lives of pre-revolution militants were intensely bound to the repertoires of external positions of the time and context in which they lived, which influenced their cultural socialisation. Such external positions underpinned the development of their personal narratives and at the same time were moulded by it. Henrique from the LUAR echoed this by giving voice to the position *I as a product of my life's external circumstances.* He felt his choices were nothing "extraordinary", just as Rita viewed her choices as "normal":

> People might say that I had great "democratic awareness". Two big words to which I can say *no*! I usually say that if I had been born

> somewhere else, in a different time, in different circumstances, I would be someone completely different. Therefore, this is not extraordinary. That's what I tell people: it is not extraordinary to be one thing or another. People react, and I think that in life we react to the circumstances.

Although both family and birthplace played central roles in the political awareness of many interviewees, it is important to highlight that a few individuals considered that this was not always the case. Diogo from the LUAR, for instance, insisted that the family factor "is not fatal", since the parents of some militants were solid supporters of the regime. Nuno from the BR confirmed this affirmation, recounting that his family was "quite closed" and

> right-wing, totally right-wing! [Laughs.] Humanists, but absolutely right-wing. Just to give you an example: in the year Salazar fell off his chair and was in a coma and everyone thought he was going to die, my birthday was a few days after that. My mother did not allow me to have a birthday party because Salazar was dying. You see, this was the family I came from.

In Nuno's case, other external and internal positions played important roles in his political awareness. He was born in Angola, one of the Portugal's African colonies at the time, and recognised that while living there he never noticed anything abnormal. Then, his parents sent him to university in Lisbon, but placed him in an Opus Dei[1] residency, which Nuno believed kept him "away from the world". However, everything changed when he returned to Luanda for a year's study and noticed how badly native Angolans were treated. At this point in time, his monological self, curated until then by external forces that leaned towards the *Estado Novo* (e.g., his parents, the Opus Dei residency), became receptive to different perspectives and centrifugal forces that generated openness to transformation and innovation. Upon his return to Portugal, he engaged in conversations regarding the situation in the colonies and developed contacts with the opposition to the *Estado Novo*. However, after attending a number of meetings, he felt frustrated. He felt that the opposition merely debated the regime, its origins, and its evolution, while he wanted to *do* something: "I wanted to solve the problem, I did not want to understand how it was created!" Subsequently, in the midst of making sense of his environment and his role within it, Nuno resolved his search for identity by adhering to the position *I as an Angolan:*

> After many conversations and much reflection I decided to become Angolan. Angola was going through the liberation struggle and I felt Angolan and I wanted to take part in the Angolan liberation struggle

> because it made a lot of sense to me. I had no doubt about it: it was about the oppression of a people.

From the moment he decided to consider himself an Angolan, he started looking for ways to assist the efforts of the liberation movement in Angola, leading to his engagement with the BR, which had a strong anti-colonial and anti-imperial component.

Pre-revolution militants: political participation and education

At a later stage, voluntary involvement with activities and events of a political nature also shaped pre-revolution militants' political awareness and helped it to reach full maturity. The *Estado Novo*, as explored in Chapter 1, did not tolerate opposition political parties or any anti-regime political activity. In this context, the political police established a secret network of informers, which created an environment of fear and avoidance of political issues. Anyone could be an informer, and any suspicion of anti-regime political activity could be harshly punished.

In this context, militants had to find creative ways to oppose the *Estado Novo*. Marco from the LUAR, for instance, considered that the uncensored newspaper coverage of the Vietnam War was quite useful in the Portuguese political environment of the 1960s, which was characterised by repression and an absence of freedom of speech: "The Vietnam War was discussed openly. It was not something that our newspapers censored much. This allowed us to discuss and follow the American crimes in Vietnam". For Marco, discussing the war in Vietnam was motivated by a sense of revenge, "because we could not discuss ours, because our crimes in Africa were always covered up". Nevertheless, ordinary Portuguese citizens "could follow our war closely, because our friends were joining it and were coming back alive or injured". Marco also mentioned the Latin American guerrillas' struggle, which was as familiar as "daily bread. It was impossible to hide them". Thus, such events, at both the national and the international level, fuelled the imagination and enriched the identity repertoires of pre-revolution militants, who, even under a repressive regime, found ways of plunging into others' experiences and making sense of their own.

University was another environment that stirred political activity during the *Estado Novo* because it allowed participation in student unions, access to new reading material, and opportunities to write. It also gave access to a new world of politicised and anti-regime individuals, who were ready to debate, recruit, and get organised. (For more on the student opposition to the regime, see Cruzeiro and Bebiano, 2006.) Thus, on the one hand, some individuals went to university and gained very solid theoretical knowledge that helped to mould their views, choices, and commitment to the struggle. Emílio from the LUAR, for instance, buttressed his militancy by adopting the position *I as a leftist theorist looking for more effective ways of fighting*:

> I read Gramsci; I was a theorist. I went to university. I did part of my studies in France; I got two Master's degrees from France and was a teacher there. I came here to do my doctorate ... in 1980. So, I was reading the theoreticians of contemporary Marxism–Leninism about the fight against historicism and the attempt to find a dialectical praxis that was a little different from the Communist Party – a party that was very crystallising for us.

On the other hand, some individuals consulted books in search of support for the views they had developed through their own life experiences. Ana from the BR, for instance, when discussing her political awareness, explained that politics was a taboo subject at home. Indeed, the first time she questioned her father about the issue, he fainted. Women and children were not supposed to question the head of the household. Consequently, while Ana's reading shaped her views, the absence of opportunities to discuss them openly always left her unsure about her beliefs. After finishing secondary school, she started working as a maid for a very wealthy family. Coming from a poor family herself, the new environment proved to be a great shock: "What is this? Wait, there are those people on that side – my parents, my parents' friends, my uncles and so on – and then there is *this* [luxury]". This questioning and eagerness to understand society and social issues remained with Ana through the years, leading her to look for answers in books:

> In regards to my theoretical basis, I had those feelings of "Now I have to go and read Marx – how awful! Now I have to read to support my feelings, because there must be a reason for all this. So, to plot against those men who are screwing us, what do we do? What must be done?" And Hegel ... I still remember the dialectic; it has stayed with me for life! And Engels ... I read and read and read to try to understand.

Thus, Ana's unique combination of identity positions, which included *I as part of an unfair society*, but also the insecurity of *I as someone who did not study politics at university* (which was the first thing she told me on the phone when I asked if I could interview her!), and the isolation of *I as someone who has nobody with whom to discuss these ideas*, created the need to start looking for support in the ideas of philosophical giants, such as Marx, Hegel, and Engels. Furthermore, the political liberalisation of the Marcelist Spring (see Chapter 1) encouraged Ana to contemplate a different society in which people would feel excited about politics and actually engage with the political world, and where the cultural position *I as a woman who is not supposed to care for politics* would be challenged.

Pre-revolution militants: the Colonial War and exile

Finally, there were two other experiences that contributed to the development of some pre-revolution militants' political awareness: participation in the

Colonial War and exile. The Colonial War worked in different ways for different interviewees. Some never participated in it directly (because they fled from Portugal into exile), but they still felt it quite closely. They lost loved ones, saw the return of physically and psychologically injured friends and relatives, and experienced social rejection for fleeing from the war and causing the soldiers in the field to suffer longer campaigns. Others had personal experience of the war. Some were forced into compulsory military service, while others chose a military career. These distinctions are important because they framed individuals' experiences and were decisive in the direction in which their political awareness developed. That said, none of the interviewees who participated in the armed struggle against the *Estado Novo* voluntarily enlisted for the Colonial War; indeed, in the majority of cases, they opposed it fiercely. Their opposition was primarily motivated by ideological stances against colonialism and imperialism, and, secondarily, by the human and economic toll the war exacted. Furthermore, first-hand participation in the Colonial War tended to solidify opposition, generating very strong antipathy towards the war itself and its architect – the regime. Xavier from the ARA, for instance, was sent to a war in which he witnessed the darkest aspects of his fellow human beings:

> The war was a terrible thing – for men and women in general. Either they already have a good education, a good political and social awareness, or they become beasts. All those values, those principles, go to pieces. The aim was to kill as much as possible.

This fuelled the radicalisation-prone position *I as someone who hates the Colonial War* and catalysed the engagement-prone position *I as someone who will make war on war*: "I came to hate the war. We used to say: 'We went to war in the service of the state and now we dedicate our lives to making war on war.' And so we did".

In the context of the ARA, another interviewee's participation in the Colonial War had a very deep impact on his political awareness and subsequent actions. Rui's reasoning was very interesting, displaying a radicalisation process that peaked with his participation in the Colonial War. He started by explaining how damaging the war was for the country and for its people, showcasing his core external position: *My country and its people as victims of a criminal regime.* This position led Rui to question the war itself and the regime that was waging it: "The Colonial War turned out to be the drop of acid that stings the eyes, causing them to open and see ... an injured country... injured in the womb, which is its people". Rui also reflected on his personal, first-hand experience of the war, echoing Xavier's positions *I as someone who hates the Colonial War* and *I as someone who will make war on war*:

> When I joined the war, I was willing to fight it both here and there. Before going, after going, and after returning, for me it was like a civic

> duty, but when I joined the war and saw what I saw … I thought that all possible limits had been exceeded and anything would be legitimate to end it. I came back with my mind made up – not only feeling very deep indignation, revulsion … but willing to do anything.

In order to illustrate what he meant by "all possible limits had been exceeded", Rui recounted a particular incident from his military service in Mozambique:

> One day I was in Nampula, in the military hospital, and a lady who looked like a cupcake arrived. She was very, very angry because one of her maids … had put her fingers in the sugar bowl, taken some sugar and put it in her mouth, defiling her sugar! The lady got a broom, and – I'm going to tell you something that you will not believe, but this is what she did – she broke the maid's arms and legs … And nothing happened to the woman! Things like this were part of my daily life, things that I would see or that others would tell me they had seen. The military were often cruel, but not gratuitously; they were violent, but less spontaneously; they were more thoughtful. The settlers, especially the settlers in the countryside, were not only very violent but also full of prejudice. There was absolute racism – irrational racism that would not make any distinction between a black person and a dog or a cat or any other wild animal! There was no distinction in terms of either dignity or nature. Look, I saw so much of it, didn't I? Therefore, I returned in a state of fury. The order that led to the implementation and perpetuation of what I saw there had to be destroyed.

Rui told this story in a very solemn tone. The woman's brutality to her maid was one of many atrocities he witnessed during two years of military service in Mozambique. Those experiences changed his life. Witnessing colonial and war atrocities made him realise that something had to be done and that he needed to play an active role. In his opinion, "almost everyone did not approve" of the sort of behaviour described in his story, "but a large number of people still approved and, more pertinently, very few people would report it or fight against it". Nevertheless, he concluded: "I was part of the latter group".

As mentioned earlier, the Colonial War also caused many young people to evade military service and flee into exile, mainly to France, Luxembourg, or Belgium. Among the organisations who fought the regime during the dictatorship, the LUAR was the one with the most militants in exile. Various interviewees described life in exile as difficult, but, at the same time, as an influential factor in the development of their political awareness. For these interviewees, the combination of being forced out of their country, the hardships of life in exile, and the opportunity to familiarise themselves with democratic societies created a sense that something needed to be done to stop what was happening in Portugal. Marco from the LUAR, for instance, sought refuge in Luxembourg, which allowed him to "make the comparison" and ask: "Why doesn't the world look like this country? Why can't we function like that?" However, he affirmed that he was unable to enjoy life in Luxembourg because he felt that he had to do something regarding the situation in Portugal:

> I felt that I did not have the right to enjoy it, you see? Unlike most people, I thought I had no right to take advantage of a society to which I had not contributed when my country needed me.

In this vein, Marco's identity system started revolving around the pro-radicalisation position *I as a young exile who has to do something regarding my country's situation*. Nevertheless, he recognised that other exiles followed different lines of thought. In fact, in his opinion, numerous exiles were strongly influenced by the Catholic Church's narratives, which were pro-regime. Thus, despite suffering severe hardship, Portuguese people abroad rarely raised their voices against the *Estado Novo*:

> Our emigration at the time was very fragile economically, but also culturally … It was fairly dominated by the priests' mentality – religion weighed people down terribly. Despite leaving Portugal clandestinely, going through dreadful circumstances to go abroad, they were still connected to the system, still attached to Mr Priest, still attached to the official policies … They never referred to the misery in Portugal and the reasons why they had fled.

In this context, Marco found his anti-regime position – which had been part of his environment while growing up and had made him choose exile over military service in the Colonial War – at odds with the conservative, pro-regime views of many of his fellow exiles. He reiterated that few exiles participated in the Portuguese opposition, and even fewer planned to take up arms and fight the dictatorship. In his view, the majority of the population had a passive attitude and just wished to live their lives, following the principles into which they had been born and bred: "Very often, theorists put our emigration in a situation of opposition … but it was not. Our emigration was, generally, subservient". Nowadays, in some circles of society, it is difficult to recognise this situation. It is far easier to look back and see strong opposition to an oppressive dictatorship. However, as Marco interestingly stated: "History is made as it is and not as we imagine it". And the "history" he experienced was punctuated by a lack of support from conservative exiles who were blind to the origin of their own hardship because they were unable to disconnect themselves from the traditional storylines created by the political narratives and myths inculcated by the *Estado Novo*.

Counter-revolution militants: family and Catholicism

The descriptions of family presented by counter-revolution militants portrayed conservative relatives who were determined to raise their children in accordance with the regime's values and ideals. Thus, their stories revolved around education based on very strict morality, steered by Catholicism and tradition. As already mentioned, this was the norm across Portuguese society, which, in general, leaned towards the regime's ideology. The majority of the population preferred to remain loyal to a regime that had created a stable and morally respectable narrative of the nation, a sense of order and control, and an image of happiness and prosperity. Despite being handed from generation to generation, all of these impressions can be opposed, as we have seen in the case of Nuno from the BR. However, they can also be used to preserve continuity, acting as centripetal forces in the self and contributing to the integration of pro-regime positions in an individual's identity repertoire.

In this context, Catholicism was highlighted as a moral compass, which, in the words of Dinis from the MDLP, "would prevent, in normal people, adherence to extremist ideologies and political systems". Thus, the dominant I-position *I as a Catholic* automatically subjugated alternatives such as *I as someone who might see the regime differently, I as someone who might challenge the regime's narratives*, or *I as someone who might want to change ideologically*, while also encouraging a centripetal movement of other I-positions around being "normal people", such as *I as a supporter of the regime* or *I as an upholder of morality and good manners.*

Counter-revolution militants: reading and political participation

If reading contributed to generating an awareness of the injustices of the regime among pre-revolution militants, for counter-revolution militants it provided stark warnings about the risk of a communist takeover in Portugal. Dinis, for instance, considered that books on "the process of the installation of communism in other countries" alerted him to the possibility of a "bloodbath" in Portugal. Similarly, Daniel, also from the MDLP, came to believe that "what happened in Russia in 1917 could happen in Portugal, too".

These political concerns proliferated in Portugal after the April Revolution and led to the founding of a number of new political parties. Two, in particular, were supported by individuals who would go on to become MDLP militants: the *Movimento Federalista Português* (Portuguese Federalist Movement) and the *Partido do Progresso* (Progress Party). The former was created to lobby for a federalist solution to the colonial problem; specifically, it advocated adoption of the British Commonwealth model. However, the independence of the colonies caused a division within this party and the consequent formation of the Progress Party. According to Daniel, a number of individuals within the Progress Party, including himself,

> thought that we should continue our political struggle no longer on the question of Africa, where there was nothing else to do, but look for a more balanced approach, which would not be too capitalist, or too socialist, but a third way.

However, in the context of the post-April Revolution turmoil, the Progress Party was banned and several of its members, including Daniel, were arrested. Consequently, during this troubled period, individuals who were perceived as leaning towards the deposed regime felt threatened and, in some cases, decided to escape to Spain and join the embryonic MDLP. Daniel was one of them, and he now believes that his decision was motivated by the fact that his "historical past" convinced him that the future of his country was threatened by communism. Subsequently, the positions generated by this "historical past", such as *I as someone under threat in my own country* and *I as a young individual who should defend my country from communism*, lay at the heart of his radicalisation process, including his politicisation and subsequent engagement with the armed struggle.

Counter-revolution militants: the Colonial War

As mentioned earlier, the Colonial War played a variety of roles in regard to raising the political awareness of different interviewees. This variety is particularly evident when comparing pre- and counter-revolution militants, who in the majority of cases belonged to a single generation but chose very different paths. Thus, the vast majority of ELP and MDLP militants were former military personnel who had either volunteered for or at least willingly participated in the Colonial War. This experience helped frame their political awareness and views on the decolonisation process triggered by the April Revolution. In this context, it is interesting to trace the experience of Afonso from the ELP, whose story features in this book's Introduction. He fought in both Angola and Mozambique, and views his African experience as a key driver of his subsequent involvement with the ELP:

> The reason behind my fight in '74/'75 [within the ELP] follows on from the two tours of duty I did in Africa. They were mostly missions in defence of the African populations and their development in relation to very, very violent armed extremist groups – the MPLA,[2] UNITA (less so),[3] FRELIMO[4] and PAIGC.[5] They all trained in the Soviet Union and in China and were based on a Soviet campaign to take control of Africa and subsequently get rid of the European countries – the so-called "decolonisation".

Throughout his interview, Afonso stressed that the Colonial War comprised "defence missions". It was about defending both the settlers and the natives from the extreme violence of the communist guerrilla movements. In this sense, Afonso's clearly dominant I-positions were *My country is fighting for its people* and *My country's enemies are the communists.* Therefore, his personal positions mirrored the political narrative on which the *Estado Novo* regime based the necessity of waging the Colonial War: the need to fight against terrorist organisations supported by international communism. Additionally, Afonso highly praised the work done by the Portuguese regime with respect to the development of the colonies, emphasising security – "in '74 you could pick up a Volkswagen and travel in Angola from one end to the other without trouble" – economic growth – "Angola was in a development boom, with a GDP growth of twelve per cent per annum during all those years" – and the military's positive contribution to the colonies' progress:

> the armed forces had a major role in the development and support of African populations: schools, hospitals, access roads, everything. Forty per cent of the armed forces' expenditure in Angola, Mozambique, and Guinea was connected to supporting the population because our strategy was never to lose the full support of the population to the communist movements.

In fact, this was the strategy of General Spínola, governor and commander-in-chief of Guinea, as summarised in his slogan "For a Better Guinea" (Antunes, 1995, p. 57). The aim of this strategy was to improve the living conditions of the local people in the hope that they would allign themselves with the Portuguese cause, to the detriment of the PAIGC, the Guinean liberation movement led by Amilcar Cabral. It was pursued not only in Guinea but in Mozambique, where, according to Afonso, a majority of the "native" soldiers had better qualifications than their Portuguese counterparts because Mozambique had a superior education system. This led Afonso to insist: "It was all consistent because we had the support of the population and we had done a brilliant development job". In this vein, his self was in perfect monologue, giving voice to the pro-regime political narratives according to which he had been raised and constantly feeding them with positive examples from his own environment. Thereby, Afonso's perspective on the Portuguese presence and activities in the various African colonies, including the Colonial War – which represents the perspectives of all of the counter-revolution interviewees – differed utterly from the pre-revolution militants' perspectives on this subject. In fact, Rui and Afonso could be considered polar opposites. This seems to be due to the distinct social, cultural, and political narrative resources that constituted their subjective experiences. While Afonso was educated to recognise and admire the positive aspects of the regime and to uphold its ideals, Rui was educated to oppose injustice and help the most vulnerable members of society. Consequently, the ways in which they perceived their pasts were totally different, as were their political grievances and the paths of action they chose.

Meanwhile, continuing Afonso's narrative, the April Revolution took place, but he never felt "that the coup in Lisbon would jeopardise the delivery of the population to the enemy". Such an outcome was unthinkable for Afonso, because he believed that the African colonies were component parts of Portugal and always would be. Hence, he was astonished when he heard news of the decolonisation process:

> General Costa Gomes went to Mozambique and stated that the power in Mozambique would be handed over to FRELIMO. Just like that. That was a tremendous shock, because we were in the bush, fighting normally, and suddenly the deputy chief of staff says: "No, we will hand over all power to the enemy".

Obviously, General Costa Gomes never explicitly stated: "We are handing all the power over to the enemy", but Afonso interpreted the decolonisation process in that way. To him, it meant betraying the people of the colonies by delivering them to "the enemy". However, his monological self prevented him from seeing that "the enemy" *were* the people of the colonies. They opposed Portuguese colonial rule and fought for independence within the liberation movements. By constructing them as "the enemy", Afonso disregarded the fact that some of the people he wished to protect did not want his protection. They wanted an independent state that was free from colonial rule.

Afonso decided to make his views on the decolonisation process public during a gathering of officers and sergeants in Mozambique. He climbed onto the stage and told everyone that proceeding with decolonisation "would be a crime of which we could not be cleansed for many generations". His speech resulted in his expulsion from Mozambique. Before leaving, he contacted the president of Rhodesia and asked him to accept his soldiers as refugees, but his request was denied. Hence, he had to leave while they stayed behind, and he grieved for them on his journey home. When talking about this watershed moment, he evoked his three core I-positions: *I as a soldier* ("captain of the paratroopers"); *I as part of a heroic family* ("son of a princess, a great heroine in the Second World War, sentenced to death twice – by the Gestapo and the Soviet NKVD"); and *I as someone who had an austere upbringing* ("I always had an austere upbringing"). These comprised the pillars of Afonso's self, his points of reference, the definers of his morality and values, the episodic particulars of his autobiographical memory that lay at the heart of his narrative identity. None of them prevented his suffering or stopped the tears from rolling from his eyes at his farewell meeting with his men, but they made a significant contribution to and motivated his subsequent militant activities.

Afonso's upbringing and subjective experiences did not allow him to accept the "betrayal", the "delivery", and the "abandonment" of the colonial population, which now faced "slaughter" by "the enemy". He felt that this constituted a crime perpetrated by the new political establishment after the April Revolution:

> The decolonisation was the final straw of 25 April. The banks being more or less nationalised … from all that, more or less, we could recover. Now,

> with two million dead Africans in Africa who trusted us? And we abandoned them to the enemy ... That is terrible!

This was the storyline that framed and justified Afonso's struggle upon his return to Portugal after the April Revolution, feeding his radicalisation and engagement-prone I-positions, just as the cruelty of the Colonial War waged by the *Estado Novo* had framed and justified Rui's struggle prior to the same revolution.

Post-revolution militants: children of the revolution

Future FP-25 militants' experienced two very different political contexts in the early stages of their lives: they were born in the last years of the *Estado Novo*, a time of some turbulence; and in their early teens that regime was overthrown, leading to a period of euphoria and politicisation that shaped their political awareness. At least one of the FP-25 militants, Humberto, explicitly saw himself through the I-position *I as a product of my life's external circumstances*: "I'm like most people – I am a product of 25 April's history, so ... I'm actually a product of the 25 April generation". According to Humberto, his politically violent militancy began only after he had experimented with legal ways of achieving socio-political transformation:

> The bulk of the people are the ones that, on one side or the other, were involved in the demonstrations, occupations, this and that, things on the streets, until they reached a point when they said: "We have had enough of all this, let's move forward".

Mariana's life experiences, which are detailed in the Introduction to this book also mirror these circumstances quite well. She reflected that a core position in her life was *I as a reactionary*. Like other militants, she placed the tales of a Republican grandfather, who was "systematically arrested", at the origin of her political awareness. Such tales gave voice to dissent-prone positions around the external position *My grandfather as part of the Republican resistance to the Estado Novo*. Despite being "born and bred in fascism", Mariana considered that, from an early age, she had access to alternative perspectives that made her challenge the *Estado Novo*'s narratives. These perspectives were conveyed by family stories, but also by censored singers and authors. Finally, Mariana adopted the position *I as someone who possesses a natural predisposition to respond to social injustice*. According to this position, she described her subsequent political journey as constant engagement with oppositional political activities against injustice. Before the April Revolution, she opposed the injustice perpetrated by the regime (e.g., assassinations conducted by the political police, the Colonial War). After the revolution, she joined the PRP/BR – the political party which developed out of the BR – and supported its members both in prison and in the underground:

> I joined the PRP in 1974, when I was sixteen years old. In the PRP I was a militant. Then there were the PRP prisoners. I worked on the connections with the prisoners, visited them in jail, facilitated their contact with the outside. I fully supported the prisoners and the people who had retreated into life underground.

Finally, she joined the FP-25 to fight what she perceived as injustices perpetrated by the right-wing against the workers.

Post-revolution militants: reading, political imagination and activism

Early reading on political matters and political events around the world was quite influential for some post-revolution militants. Duarte, for instance, who was connected with the PRP/BR after the revolution and later worked with the ideological branch of the FP-25, described his ongoing curiosity and thirst for knowledge while growing up. He came from a remote village in one of the Portuguese archipelagos, and the first books he bought formed part of a "sociological anthology" written by a Portuguese author, António Sérgio, who was influenced by Nordic corporatism and social democracy. Duarte acknowledged that "there were many things I did not understand [at the time]. I was very young, but I kept trying to understand". His commitment to social democracy, the defence of freedom, and pedagogy was eventually challenged by news of the Cuban Revolution and increasing exposure to other authors, including Lenin and the Brazilian Jorge Amado, whose books circulated discreetly in Portugal despite the regime's attempts to ban them. These alternative ideas led Duarte to the conclusion that "in Portugal, it was impossible to eradicate fascism through pacifism … The route of violence was needed, the armed struggle". Thus, some years later, when he moved to Lisbon to study, he felt that his I-position *I as a leftist individual* crystallised: "Before coming to study in Lisbon, I had done all this reading. So, when I came here, I already had a leftist position".

In this vein, all of the FP-25 militants were surrounded by a revolutionary culture and revolutionary political narratives, which were based not only in Portugal but all around the world. This generation of militants admired the revolutionary figures of their time and had a specific way of interpreting their behaviour. However, in some cases, that interpretation changed over time, as Humberto explained:

> the Spanish Revolution, the Cuban Revolution, the armed struggles in Africa, and so on. Even in my case, I did not live it, but I met people who did. I met people who took part in the Spanish Revolution. I don't think I met people from Russia, but I met people who fought in the African liberation movements and that created a picture in your mind … Today, you look at the MPLA and laugh, don't you? However, I am from a generation that looks at Amilcar Cabral[6] with

> respect and sees people who fought against the Portuguese – small groups that were fighting against a powerful colonial army – many of them left everything to go and fight for the independence of the colonies and so on. I mean we had a different idea: you would see people who were part of the PRP, of the LUAR, of the PCP, who were in France preparing the armed struggle, and so on. So, we come from this culture of people, some a little older than us, some quite a bit older, but people who think that [change can be achieved] only through armed revolution … This is a totally different culture.

Humberto felt that the external voices of foreign and national resistance movements, revolutions, and fighters played a significant role in his political imagination. Such an influence of shared political narratives was fairly consistent across the post-revolution militants' personal narratives, and strongly shaped their political awareness, identity, and action. This, in conjunction with their perception of the events that took place in the early years of democracy in Portugal, drove FP-25 militants to reflect on the path they had chosen, which was absolutely legal at first and only later – after all their dreams had been shattered – became clandestine and violent.

Júlia's case serves as a fine example of this process. As a young adult, she experienced the euphoria of a revolution that brought forty-eight years of dictatorship to an end. This social context seems to have empowered her social-intervention-prone position, *I as an idealist looking for social transformation*:

> It was the moment when all social norms were called into question, all political choices were questioned and we were part of that in a very intense way … It was little more than the idea that we were all equal and that we could create a society in which people were all equal.

It was difficult to integrate this I-position with the one that was culturally established for a young Portuguese woman at that moment in time – *I as a future wife and mother* – as we shall explore in the next two chapters. However, in Júlia's case, the *I as an idealist looking for social transformation* position assumed a dominant role and she became increasingly involved in political activism. When she turned sixteen and left secondary school, she decided to start working in a factory because she believed that "the revolution was going to happen and it would happen in the factories". Thus, the euphoria and politicisation of the post-revolution period in Portugal helped Júlia to develop a consciousness that shaped her political awareness and framed her subsequent activities. The fact that she had some politically engaged left-wing peers, and came into contact with former violent militants who had fought the dictatorship, reinforced this process: "I got involved progressively [in legal political activity], I had some contacts, not within the organisation, simply friendships and close relationships in secondary school with people from the so-called 'extreme left'". However, Júlia and her peers saw many of the promises of the revolution overturned in the counter-revolution of 25 November 1975, creating a sense of disenchantment and shattered dreams. When discussing this, Júlia adopted the voice of the collective and listed some of the April Revolution's main achievements between 25 April 1974 and 25 November 1975, a period when she felt the socialist dream was almost realised in Portugal:

> The dream almost became reality, almost, almost … The perception that we almost took control was very strong. The fact that the military were supporting the little people … not to mention the agrarian reform, the self-management of companies, the occupation of houses, the occupation of certain companies, and so on. All that created a sense of power … that the power was ours.

The dream consisted of a strong political narrative of empowerment of the "little people", supporting the collective voice *We as the little people who are supported by the military.* During the previous regime, these people had been unable to participate in political activities without suffering harsh consequences. So, when Júlia employed the collective "we" – "The perception that *we* almost took control was very strong" – she was talking about everyone who tried to take the destiny of the country into their own hands after the April Revolution. These individuals felt that their involvement – whether big or small – had the potential to promote social change.

Commitment to a politically violent organisation

Not every Portuguese citizen who developed oppositional political awareness – either during the dictatorship or after the April Revolution – took the step of committing to politically violent militancy. Moreover, contrasting political directions were taken by those who did. This speaks directly to the caveats raised at the beginning of this chapter regarding the radicalisation process: it is not criminal in itself and it does not always lead to the commission of violent acts.

Committing to a politically violent organisation was described as a process that occurred over time and was influenced by the interaction of specific contextual factors. The interaction was crucial because, at times, a single factor might generate very different reactions. The dictatorial regime, for example, shaped politically aware people who committed themselves to fighting it (e.g., militants who joined the LUAR, the ARA and the BR), as well as politically aware people who committed themselves to defending it (e.g., militants who joined the ELP and the MDLP). In this section, I show that engagement-prone identity positions are influenced not only by the political awareness that develops in the early years of life, but also by former militants' perceptions of the political establishment of the time. Such perceptions seem to have contributed to the development of a sense of agency and to a conviction that violent action was necessary to bring about socio-political transformation.

Pre-revolution militants: justification for the armed struggle

The struggle waged by pre-revolution militants was steered by three different aims: weaken the regime; disrupt the Colonial War; and convince people that it was possible to resist and foment political change. Thus, according to Lídia from the BR, the commission of armed acts was "important from the point of view of the creation of an environment that weakens the power ... An armed act jeopardises the power because the power does not control it". This power was slaughtering the nation's sons through the "Colonial War machine", which Artur from the ARA felt "was the most notable political event of the time". The war was the beacon of the regime, the symbol of imperialism and colonialism, but also the symbol of repression, violence, and loss. It was a symbol that pre-revolution militants felt they had to exploit, not only to undermine the regime but also to raise people's awareness and convince them that they could be instruments of change.

These militants shared Rui's position: *My country and its people as victims of a criminal regime.* Rui believed that the *Estado Novo* was not as violent as German Nazism or Spanish or Italian fascism, because "the context did not allow it ... the context did not require it". Nevertheless, from his perspective, "absolutely evil" events did take place during the *Estado Novo* regime. Therefore, Rui perceived the *Estado Novo* as a "terrorist power", applying a label that is usually attached to non-state actors to a state. He felt that the Portuguese state terrorised its own people by employing extreme levels of repressive violence, which made its agents look like "wild beasts":

> The state was seen as a structure captured by an ideology ... The state was at the service of a regime, not at the service of a people or a nation, but at the service of a captured regime ... The state was a terrorist power of the monopolies; it was not a democratic power; it was not even an authoritarian power. It was a terrorist power because they attacked like wild beasts. In some places things happened in which the attacker was indistinguishable from a beast; things characterised by folly, cruelty, a lack of humanity.

This view of the *Estado Novo* regime not only justified a general need for armed struggle, but was also accompanied by a strong sense of personal duty, of being called to make a difference, which hit a generation that felt the burden of more than forty years of an oppressive regime. For pre-revolution militants, as Lídia from the BR stated, deciding to engage with a politically violent organisation was a matter of dignity: "I go because my dignity forces me to". It was a matter of being sufficiently courageous to leave one's comfort zone and risk everything to weaken the regime, as Henrique from the LUAR affirmed:

"I engaged with the struggle against Salazar because he did not allow me to fight him with the same weapons … My weapons were my courage, my decision and my willingness to risk my life". It was a matter of *I as someone who has to do what has to be done*, as Rita explained in the previous section.

Very difficult choices had to be made in this process, such as leaving one's family. Henrique, for instance, had to negotiate the conflict between the I-positions *I as a father* and *I as someone who believes that risking my life is the only way to fight the regime*. The first of these – the voice of a family man – forced him to consider the consequences of engaging in the armed struggle: "When I walked into Santa Maria [the action that preceded the formation of the LUAR], I had two young kids and I pondered: 'Well, here are my two kids, two kids that may suffer as a consequence of my attitude.'" However, the second voice – the voice of necessary risk in the context of the armed struggle – kept reminding him that if nobody was prepared to fight, no child would ever be free of oppression:

> And here is the great story: either you think of your two kids or you think of *everybody*'s kids … If nobody thinks about other people's kids and they act only when thinking about their own, this situation will never be solved.

Thus, at this major turning point in his life, Henrique found a meta-position that allowed him to live with himself as a father while plunging into the armed struggle: *I as someone who is fighting for everybody's children*. In this sense, what he identified as "the great story" was the way in which he reviewed his past and reworked it into a more bearable reality – a reality in which he sacrificed his relationship with his own children for the greater good. Through "the great story", Henrique established the value of his political choices, built a bridge between his inner world and the world outside, and managed to turn a complex reality into a set of events that he could grasp, while maintaining the integrity and coherence of his identity system.

Counter-revolution militants: justification for the armed struggle

According to Ilídio, co-founder of the MDLP, the post-April Revolution government "was very much illegal", because "no one elected them". For him, the government was "neither in nor out of the law, but above it". He also criticised the revolution itself: first, he believed that all "revolutions are imposed"; and, second, he considered that Portugal's specifically leftist revolution was against the nature of the Portuguese people, who are "a traditional people, connected to the land, Catholic". He insisted: "Nobody knew what the revolutionary movement was. Even today, I don't know what the revolutionary movement is, and I am not sure that I will ever learn". Other counter-revolution militants, such as Sérgio, also from the MDLP, voiced similar criticism. He believed that the April Revolution was unnecessary for the evolution to democracy:

> Some people say that if the revolution had not happened, we would not have democracy in Portugal today. [But] it is evident that we would, and for years, because it is evolution … Everyone used to say that the Soviet Union would never fall, but it did fall. They all fall. All empires have fallen. Everything falls.

However, counter-revolution militants were most alarmed by what they called the "undemocratic acceleration in Portugal", which began after 25 April 1974 and culminated on 11 March 1975 (the date of a failed coup launched by General Spínola, the leader of the conservative forces and later head of the MDLP; see Chapter 1). According to Daniel from the MDLP: "This acceleration was compatible with democratic elections, but those elections were held under very strong political conditioning … Therefore, we had a tutored democracy". The tutors in question were members of the Revolutionary Council, which was mostly composed of leftist military personnel who had participated in the April Revolution. Daniel explained that the Council had wide-ranging powers, conferred by the new constitution, especially by a particular article "which said that the military had the mission of ensuring the peaceful and pluralistic transition to socialism". Therefore, according to Daniel, Portugal was set on an exclusively socialist course: "What was not acceptable was that a party would win the elections and say: 'Now, we want to stop socialism'. Here the armed forces had a constitutional duty to intervene". In this vein, Daniel continued: "After 11 March in Portugal there was no democracy, make no mistake … In the period from March 1975 to November 1975, the real situation in Portugal was that things happened that had nothing to do with democracy". Thus, he insisted that anyone who disagreed with the Revolutionary Council was subjected to "warrantless arrests", "popular trials", "simulated executions", and periods in "jail without talking with a lawyer". He also mentioned the state's control of the media and the "increasing weight of the Communist Party", which led counter-revolution militants to the belief that they were "gradually walking towards a totalitarian state". Hence, violent action was necessary. The revolution had turned the Portuguese political environment to the left and the country was at serious risk of falling under a communist dictatorship, which Daniel considered "tougher, worse, make no mistake. The communist dictatorships were always much worse than Salazar's dictatorship. The human rights violations that occurred in Eastern Europe were always worse than the worst times under Salazar. What was coming was much worse".

Consequently, counter-revolution militants' decisions to commit to politically violent organisations originated from fiercely anti-communist I-positions, which, according to Sérgio from the MDLP, were "strongly influenced by the dominant culture at the time". This was a culture dominated by Cold War political narratives that depicted communism as evil – an ideology that could turn people into wild beasts, thirsty for power and world domination – as Álvaro from the MDLP affirmed:

> I was always very afraid of believing in dogmas and I always knew that Stalin was one of the greatest criminals in history. He killed six million Russians and destroyed Russia. He looted and killed so many millions of people because he was possessed by power.

It was within this "culture" that counter-revolution militants perceived the PCP's participation in Portuguese political life as a serious threat that might result in the "implementation of a communist regime in the country", as Ilídio explained. According to Afonso from the ELP, that communist participation included "the nationalisation of the whole banking system, large industries and large agricultural properties, and almost total control of radio, television, and the newspapers". He also believed that the PCP pursued "a policy of terror", which stifled the resistance of almost every Portuguese citizen:

> What was happening was that the Portuguese people, who were not communist, were afraid. They were afraid because they thought that the PCP had the majority and ruled all, because that was the image presented by the PCP: "The people are with us and we will never be defeated". Then, we had to prove that the PCP was a minority, that the PCP could be frightened, if necessary, and that the majority of the Portuguese people was not communist.

Thus, counter-revolution militants constructed the PCP and its members as "the enemy" by holding fast to the cultural positions of the deposed regime in which they had been raised: *My country and its people as Catholic*, which automatically meant *My country and its people as anti-communist*. Such positions were strengthened by perceptions of the significance of the Catholic Church in Portugal, which Sérgio described as "a Church that comes from the old regime". Ilídio added that the Church would have raised "a popular army" to fight the "red invasion" if necessary. Therefore, action had to be taken to stop communism and the communists from damaging the country and to strengthen the Portuguese people's voice by affirming, as Afonso put it: "We are the majority and we have the right to choose, not an active minority, violent and armed like the PCP".

Post-revolution militants: justification for the armed struggle

Six years after the revolution, the militants of the FP-25 felt that violent action was required to achieve their "ideological conception". As Duarte explained: "The armed struggle was an indispensable element of the mass struggle, together with intervention in the unions, in various places". The armed struggle "was the driving force and the radicalisation" of the mass struggle. Moreover, according to Jaime, FP-25's militants felt that "violence was a weapon" that could be used "according to the political analysis of a certain situation". In this vein, if political analysis identified severe injustice and inequality in the social fabric, "violence was a weapon in the workers' hands to show their revolt". Therefore, various FP-25 militants displayed the I-position *I as a fighter against social injustice*. This position is associated with the perception that social injustice is the inevitable result of an unfair capitalist state machine, which, in the words of Júlia, "exists to protect capitalists". Consequently, the I-position *I as a militant who perceives violence as necessary* was also prevalent, because violent actions perpetrated against capitalist symbols were seen as an effective means of halting the capitalist machine and reversing the unequal distribution of resources. Júlia exemplified these I-positions:

> I believe that the political confrontation in certain situations goes through processes of violence, and often violence that comes from only one side … In our case, though, the process was from both sides, because when you leave people without solutions for life, you are using violence, even if such violence is passively accepted and the people applying it are not targeted by social criticism or repudiated by society. However, for me, they are obviously using completely antisocial behaviour because holding the means of production does not mean that you can do whatever you wish – buy Ferraris instead of investing in companies and then throw away the garbage that is the workers … So, I believe that social conflict is not absolutely reprehensible.

In this sense, for post-revolution militants, the decision to join a politically violent organisation originated in disappointment with the political path taken by the country after the April Revolution. As Jaime explained, in this period, the political establishment was "again opening the doors to the people who had ruled the country for years". It was as if the capitalist families went on holiday for a few years, but then returned to reclaim their previous exalted places in society. In this vein, for FP-25's militants, the democracy of the late 1970s was no more than "formal democracy". It allowed people to vote but merely "protected the dominant classes". This was anathema to these militants' anti-capitalistic, socialist principles. In this socio-political landscape, the post-revolution militants chose to embrace armed-struggle-prone I-positions. Thus, Júlia affirmed that "a choice was internalised", involving "an active response in relation to the advances of the right". Meanwhile, Bruno believed that the FP-25

> appeared in the context of a major assault from the right in order to articulate some more radical ways of struggle and to show the workers

that when certain forms of struggle are exhausted, there are other means of responding to the arrogance of capital, there are other ways of acting.

Conclusion

In this chapter, I have demonstrated how families and birthplaces played central roles in establishing the principles and beliefs that most former militants nurtured. The connections between these former militants and the people around them, as well as the cultural meanings of their environment, crafted their identity repertoires. In this context, it is no wonder that we find positions such as *My family as traditionally part of the resistance, My father as an agent of my political awareness*, and *My grandfather as part of the Republican resistance to the Estado Novo.* Such external positions represented valued family members' characteristics that were integrated within the former militants' selves, giving meaning to who they were and how they saw themselves and their place in the world.

The influence of these personal early life contexts was apparent when some former militants faced the socio-political turmoil of the Colonial War. Pre-revolution militants raised in strongly anti-regime environments populated by oppositional political narratives, who were sent to fight in the Colonial War, perceived it as the heyday of atrocities committed by the *Estado Novo* regime. For these militants, participation in the war generated radicalisation-prone I-positions, such as *I as someone who hates the Colonial War*, which in turn encouraged engagement-prone positions, such as *I as someone who will make war on war*. In this sense, the pre-revolution militants' justifications for their armed struggle were linked not only to their perceptions of the *Estado Novo* as a repressive and violent dictatorial regime, but also to their views and experiences of the Colonial War. These circumstances led various pre-revolution militants to share the external position *My country and its people as victims of a criminal regime*. However, this was not just an abstract standpoint but a position that led individuals to organise their lives according to a plan to engage with a politically violent organisation.

In the case of counter-revolution militants, raised by regime supporters and fervent Catholics, the Colonial War was seen in a totally different light. For these militants, it was about defending Portuguese people and territory, as reflected in the external positions *My country is fighting for its people* and *My country's enemies are the communist liberation movements*, and the internal position *I as a member of the military*. However, this latter position was not automatically abandoned after the April Revolution. Counter-revolution militants could not come to terms with the decolonisation process that was launched by the post-revolution political establishment. In their opinion, this was a crime that challenged their education, ideological principles, and moral values. Moreover, counter-revolution militants felt that their lives and freedom were threatened by the post-revolution political establishment. They feared, in particular, the implementation of a communist regime in Portugal.

Consequently, engagement-prone positions started to emerge, such as *I as a young individual who should defend my country from communism*. Thus, these militants justified armed action on the basis of the need to restore order and stop a communist takeover in Portugal on behalf of a Catholic country (*My country and its people as Catholic*) which was not communist (*My country and its people as anti-communist*).

Finally, post-revolution militants, born in the last couple of decades of the *Estado Novo* regime, built a narrative identity by seeing themselves as "products" of the revolution and the intense political activity and political narratives that surrounded it: *I as a product of my life's external circumstances.* They were inspired by earlier militants who had fought against Portugal's oppressive regime, and by other militants around the world, such as African liberation movements and Latin American guerrillas. This fed their narrative imagination and helped them to situate their personal experiences and ways of acting, giving rise to such I-positions as *I as a leftist individual* and *I as an idealist looking for social transformation.*

The post-revolution militants' justifications for their armed struggle were related to the events that took place in Portugal after the 25 November 1975 counter-revolution. This shattered all of their socialist dreams and restored an order that gradually returned everything and everyone to their former places in society. In this socio-political context, there were fears of a return of the authoritarian political establishment and an erosion of the April Revolution's achievements. The latter could be seen through, for instance, increasing discrimination against the working class. In this environment, the identity systems of post-revolution militants started to be centred on pro-engagement positions, such as *I as a fighter against social injustice* and *I as a militant who perceives violence as necessary.* These I-positions highlighted the need to fight back against social injustice, reassert the socialist promises of the April Revolution, and achieve socio-political transformation.

Thus, in this chapter, I have substantiated the findings of a number of previous studies regarding the complex radicalisation process that leads to engagement with a politically violent organisation (see, e.g., McCauley and Moskalenko, 2008; Ashour, 2009). In this vein, I have traced the personal and contextual factors underpinning former militants' identity systems, which led to their conviction that armed action was necessary to initiate socio-political transformation. Therefore, former militants did not simply engage with politically violent organisations independently of the political narratives and experiences that populated their life stories. On the contrary, they used those stories, and those of the people around them, to justify their militancy. They crafted internal positions that gave meaning to who they were in the contexts they inhabited, such as *I as someone who possesses a natural predisposition to respond to social injustice.* Yet, they also integrated aspects of these contexts in their own selves through external positions, such as *My family as traditionally part of the resistance* or *My country is fighting for its people.* Nevertheless, at critical moments, many former militants felt the battle among conflicting

I-positions: for instance, the voice of the family encapsulated by the counter-engagement position *I as a father* against the voice of fighting for freedom represented by the pro-engagement position *I as someone who believes that risking my life is the only way to fight the regime.* Different routes were taken to solve such conflicts and attain a stable narrative identity (see Chapter 2 for details). For instance, the militant who was torn between his counter- and pro-engagement positions ultimately threw a meta-position into the mix – *I as someone who is fighting for everybody's children* – which allowed him to live with himself as an absent father who was fighting for the greater good.

In Chapter 4, I explore the dynamics of life within a politically violent organisation. The existing literature has rarely explored these dynamics, meaning there is a gap in our knowledge relating to what happens between engagement with and disengagement from a politically violent organisation. This gap brings to mind Cynthia Mahmood's comment that we do not know enough about politically violent militants to engage with them effectively, as we tend to ignore what often amounts to several years of their lives (Mahmood, 1996).

Notes

1 Opus Dei, formally known as the Prelature of the Holy Cross and Opus Dei, is an institution of the Roman Catholic Church which teaches that everyone is called to holiness and that ordinary life is a path to sanctity. It comprises lay members and priests who observe standard spiritual practices, such as daily mass, rosary, spiritual reading and prayer, as well as specific Opus Dei prayers and customs.
2 *Movimento para a Libertação de Angola* (Movement for the Liberation of Angola).
3 *União Nacional para a Independência Total de Angola* (National Union for the Total Independence of Angola).
4 *Frente de Libertação de Moçambique* (Mozambique's Liberation Front).
5 *Partido Africano para a Independência da Guiné e de Cabo Verde* (African Party for the Independence of Guinea and Cape Verde).
6 Amilcar Cabral led the liberation movement of Guinea-Bissau and Cape Verde and the opposition forces in the ensuing war of independence in Guinea-Bissau. He was assassinated on 20 January 1973, about eight months before Guinea-Bissau's unilateral declaration of independence.

References

Antunes, J. (1995) *A guerra de África 1961–1974, Volume I.* Lisbon: Círculo de Leitores.

Ashour, O. (2009) *The de-radicalization of jihadists: transforming armed Islamist movements.* New York: Routledge.

Bjørgo, T. and Horgan, J. (2009) *Leaving terrorism behind: individual and collective disengagement.* New York: Routledge.

Brockmeier, J. (2009) 'Reaching for meaning: human agency and the narrative imagination', *Theory and Psychology*, 19(2), pp. 213–233.

Cruzeiro, M. and Bebiano, R. (2006) *Anos inquietos: vozes do movimento estudantil em Coimbra (1961–1974).* Porto: Edições Afrontamento.

della Porta, D. (2013) *Clandestine political violence.* Cambridge: Cambridge University Press.

Expert Group on Violent Radicalisation (2008) *Radicalisation processes leading to acts of terrorism, report to the European Commission.* Available at: www.rikcoolsaet.be/files/art_ip_wz/Expert%20Group%20Report%20Violent%20Radicalisation%20FINAL.pdf (accessed 30 June 2012).

Frank, A. (2010) *Letting stories breathe.* Chicago: University of Chicago Press.

Mahmood, C. (1996) *Fighting for faith and nation: dialogues with Sikh militants.* Philadelphia: University of Pennsylvania Press.

McCauley, C. and Moskalenko, S. (2008) 'Mechanisms of political radicalization: pathways toward terrorism', *Terrorism and Political Violence,* 20(3), pp. 415–433.

Taylor, M. and Horgan, J. (2006) 'A conceptual framework for addressing psychological process in the development of the terrorist', *Terrorism and Political Violence,* 18(4), pp. 585–601.

Taylor, M. and Horgan, J. (2012) 'A conceptual framework for addressing psychological process in the development of the terrorist', in Horgan, J. and Braddock, K. (eds) *Terrorism studies: a reader.* London: Routledge, pp. 130–144.

4 Life within a politically violent organisation

> This is a huge psychological game … so, if people begin to think that they are being followed, they are in fact being followed, in their imagination. While underground, I've been in situations in which my picture was in front of me in a police station and nobody identified me. In another situation, my picture was in the newspapers and on television and I was in a café and nobody recognised me. Obviously, in these circumstances, a guy has to keep calm and cold-blooded. Then, you have to have huge psychological balance; if you start to think that you are being followed, you always see shadows … It is obvious that psychologically there are moments of panic, right? … It is not easy, of course, we are always on a knife-edge: "Did they recognise me? Did they not?" The big problem is to start imagining that you were recognised. Then there are the noises. You hear a lot more than what is out there. Then there are things you must do: you *never* turn your back to the door in a restaurant. This is part of the underground manual; this is part of the novelists' literature. Sometimes it's no use, but you must do it. And then you must be careful not to be betrayed, right?
>
> (Hélder from the FP-25)

The lack of academic interest in the daily lives of politically violent militants is striking. The literature on political violence provides a wealth of information on how and why people engage with and disengage from politically violent organisations, but very little on how they actually live as committed militants. What are the dynamics of life underground? What are the challenges of being a member of a clandestine organisation? How are these manifested at the individual level? How are they felt and rationalised by different militants? What role do they play within their identity systems? For Hélder, it was all "a huge psychological game" that required "huge psychological balance". In fact, as I argue in this chapter, it demands adaptation of the whole repertoire of identity positions around the core position *I as a committed militant*.

One of the few scholars who addresses this issue in some depth is Donatella della Porta, who sees commitment to an underground politically violent organisation "as a continuation of the slippery slope that had brought activists to join the organisation" (della Porta, 2013, p. 243). She suggests two characteristics of life within a politically violent organisation that fuel both continued commitment and violence: affective and cognitive closure. The former represents the deep and intense relationships that occur among the members of a usually small, closed, restricted and restrictive organisation. This usually deepens as actions become more dangerous, casualties are incurred (e.g., the death and/or arrest of comrades), and militants do not imagine their lives differently, devoting everything they have and are to the organisation. Consequently, affective closure contributes to the dance of I-positions that construct the militant's identity, to the strengthening of solidarity with other militants, and to the increasing perception of opponents as evil or even non-human, which may prompt organisations and individuals to escalate the level of violence in their actions. Cognitive closure relates to militants' need to make sense of their behaviour. However, this invariably occurs in a constrained environment, which over time becomes tendentiously more isolated from the outside world, impacting the militants' narratives and value systems.

Therefore, life within a politically violent organisation causes transformations within individual lives and identity systems. These transformations are often products of the type of life militants need to follow underground, which in some cases implies accepting and even participating in actions that the militants themselves consider wrong or criminal (e.g., bank robberies, assassinations). However, whenever a militant leaves the underground, they can hardly return to their previous life without facing arrest, which converts ideological choices into restrictive consequences of their prior actions, firming their investment in sustaining a militant identity.

In this chapter, I address the identity positions and narratives that surround the past experience of being a committed militant in the context of a politically violent organisation. I also focus on the processes of affective and cognitive closure described by della Porta (2013), since these are intimately connected with the creation and maintenance of militants' identity repertoires. My intention in emphasising this stage in the life of a militant is to shed light on the meaning-making processes that motivate individuals to remain in a politically violent organisation. As, at this stage, militants' lives are framed by their membership of an organisation, I am able to explore not only macro- and micro-political narratives but also the meso-level – the voices of the organisations themselves. Thus, I look closely at the process of going underground, the challenges posed by life within a politically violent organisation, the relationships among the militants, the gender dynamics, the thoughts and emotions relating to committing violent acts, and the perceptions of supporters of their causes. The chapter is organised into two main sections: the dynamics of life underground and the use of violence.

The dynamics of life underground

This topic encompasses three different areas: going underground; the challenges of underground life; and gender dynamics. Its relevance is based on the fact that life within the studied organisations was often lived underground. In some cases, this life was chosen voluntarily; in other cases, it was forced upon individuals who had been identified by the police. Either way, going underground shaped militants' lives, attitudes, choices, and opportunities.

The interviewees experienced life underground in a variety of ways: some lived there for many years, others for no more than a few months; some made a total break with their former lives, others maintained contact with a few loved ones. In the case of militants who escaped underground life, they were able to pursue "normal lives" (e.g., jobs, family routines) and militancy within the organisation simultaneously, without identification by the police. These are some of the aspects of underground life that will be brought to light and discussed in the context of different sociopolitical moments.

Life underground was often represented as challenging, which is why the difficulties experienced and recounted by former clandestine militants are presented in this section, to illustrate their daily routines as part of a politically violent organisation. Militants across a variety of organisations reflected on how they coped with cutting ties with significant others, how they related to one another, the circumstances that generated interpersonal conflicts, how power relations were addressed, how militants managed to cope with high levels of stress (a consequence of participating in illegal activities and being constantly on the run from the police), and how closed and fragmented organisations produced militants who could easily lose touch with what was happening in regular society.

Finally, the gender dynamics of life underground is an equally pertinent topic to contemplate, from both male and female perspectives. These dynamics were deeply influenced by the dominant cultural storylines of the time, which specifically framed the participation and role of women within politically violent organisations. Each organisation had its own take on gender issues, ranging from a liberationist approach (e.g., the BR and some militants in the FP-25) to excluding any significant female participation in the struggle (e.g., the ELP and the MDLP).

Pre-revolution militants: going underground

Artur, one of the ARA's co-founders, chose to go underground voluntarily, before he was identified by the police. However, he made this decision only after receiving a second invitation from the PCP in 1964. The first invitation had come two years earlier, but he had considered it totally inappropriate because, as a young person, he was more focused on sorting out his personal life: "I had a life in front of me, right? I had my degree, a girlfriend … all those things, right?" In 1962, Artur's identity system was dominated by professional and relational I-positions, including *I as a student* and *I as a boyfriend*, which were culturally adequate for him at that age. However, over the next two years, his involvement with the PCP deepened, generating a different

I-position: *I as someone who believes that armed action is needed to assist the overthrow of the dictatorship*. This resulted in his decision to go underground, which was motivated by the voices that populated his surroundings. These were voices of repression, connected to a context characterised by a regime that had been in power for more than thirty years, had refused to allow any form of political choice, and had violently repressed any dissidents. However, even with this context in mind, Artur still viewed going underground as "a very violent thing" that would completely disrupt his life:

> It was a very difficult decision in my life because I knew what I was getting involved in, and what I was leaving behind – my family, all my friends, not friendship in itself, but relationships with people, leaving my degree unfinished … Well, it would be a radical change in my life.

One I-position – *I as a student* – proved especially difficult to subjugate. He mentioned the "unfinished degree" several times during the course of our interview, using it as an example of the "incredible restrictions" imposed by life underground, and as one of the long-term consequences of choosing such a path. As he explained: "At that time, having a degree, particularly being an engineer, meant having a good job and a happy life", In contrast, going underground meant "scientific and cultural limitations" and the collapse of any "professional perspectives". Looking back at that time with the benefit of hindsight, Artur insisted that the clandestine period of his life was not "unpleasant" in itself. However, he acknowledged that it had a detrimental effect on his professional life, because it prevented him from attaining his degree.

To resolve the conflict between two valued I-positions – *I as a student* and *I as someone who believes that armed action is needed to assist the overthrow of the dictatorship* – Artur opted for dominance reversal. He chose to listen to the call of his context and subjugate his personal plans. In the process, a number of centripetal forces helped him to integrate his choice of going underground within his identity system. These were exemplified by the I-positions *I as a martyr hero* and *I as one of the few people who is prepared to fight the regime*. These may be considered third positions because they acted as mediators between Artur's two conflicting I-positions.

The following story reveals how Artur made sense of his commitment to a clandestine organisation. He embarked on a process of cognitive closure, rationalising his choice by assuming a martyr–hero identity and convincing himself that he was making personal sacrifices for the greater good:

> In all wars, there is always one of those heroes, a martyr–hero, who instantly throws himself onto the grenade that is about to blow up to save the fifteen or twenty comrades who are fighting around him. So, these things are highly dependent on context, aren't they?

Therefore, Artur represents all of the militants from pre-revolutionary organisations who volunteered for life underground to build and extend the work of politically violent organisations, with the ultimate goal of overthrowing the dictatorship. Their stories are rather different from those of interviewees who were identified by the police as dissidents. The latter were forced to choose between four options: arrest and possible torture; turn informant and denounce their comrades; flee into exile; or go underground. In this sense, Lídia, who co-founded the BR, viewed going underground as "a necessary evil", since "nobody likes to do the underground work, the risk is always there, the risk of being arrested is always there … there are only disadvantages". Conversely, a "normal life" was less likely to suffer police interference and was more effective, because the limitations of underground life did not apply.

Pre-revolution militants: challenges

The most frequently cited challenge of underground life was the absence of contact with family members. Every militant agreed that it was impossible to live underground and keep in touch with family and friends. Attempting to do so would have been far too dangerous for both the militant and the people they were trying to contact. The latter might be arrested and tortured by the political police, even if they did not know anything about their relative's activities. In this sense, Henrique believed that "there can be no infidelity if you're married to the fight and to freedom". Yet, Artur and Rita from the ARA lived as a couple underground and even had two children. However, according to Rita, this was extremely difficult and there were moments of "despair". On the one hand, their youngest child had asthma and during one attack Rita feared that the little girl would die at home. On the other hand, the couple were always aware that their children would be relocated as soon as they reached school age, which was standard practice among PCP militants who assumed clandestine identities, and they both considered this "a terrible thing". However, fortunately for the couple and their children, the April Revolution intervened, as Rita explained:

> When the children reached school age they had to go somewhere. Either they would go to the Soviet Union, which happened to many and always ended very badly – the children were separated from their parents and then, in several cases, did not want to be with their parents anymore – or they went to live with family, grandparents, which was more usual … If it wasn't for 25 April, such a thing would have happened to us … It's one of the most terrible things, for sure.

The couple were extremely relieved that the revolution arrived before they had to make such a difficult decision, because once again cognitive closure processes and centripetal forces were at work in these militants' lives, feeding the I-position *I as a committed militant* while subjugating their identity systems' more personal and relational I-positions, such as *I as a mother* and *I as a father*. In this vein, it is possible to say that *I as a committed militant* became a core position in Artur's and Rita's identity systems, dictating the movements and functions of their other I-positions. Moreover, in Rita's case, the subjugation of family-related I-positions by commitment-prone I-positions – and particularly by the core position *I as a committed militant* – had previously been enacted by her own parents. They had left her with her grandparents to work under clandestine identities for the PCP, as described in the previous chapter. Thus, as her own parents had made such a sacrifice, she felt that she could – and should – do the same.

There were other challenges of underground life in the interpersonal relationships and dynamics among militants. In the case of pre-revolution militants, the relationships within each organisation were almost always described as positive, albeit limited and very constrained for security reasons. The militants did not know everyone in their respective organisations, only those with whom they conducted operations, and even then they would not share personal details. In this way, they would be protected if any of their comrades were caught and tortured by the political police. However, this seemed to contribute to the affective closure among militants, creating a deep sense of complicity and strong bonds of affection, because the militants felt that they were "taking risks together", as Lídia from the BR explained.

In order to delve deeper into this process of affective closure and to understand how militants could develop such high levels of trust in each other without forging strong personal ties beforehand, I attempted to identify the I-positions that served as pillars for this trust. They were revealed by this exchange with Rui from the ARA:

RUI: I did not know them, but the fact of meeting them in those circumstances made me assume that trust – assume that they already deserved that trust. Moreover, a clandestine [militant] today, but especially at that time, had for me a certain aura of an exceptional person … which could often be mistaken for a certain degree of heroism. If there was someone to whom I would give anything, my liver if need be, it would be that person …

INTERVIEWER: So you did not question this issue of trust or …

RUI: We did, by being aware that in that regime someone living underground had to be a militant of the highest credibility who had consciously adopted a life of hardship, sacrifice and risk. Thus, a hero … [or] in the Church context someone who would be a martyr or a saint. Since it was not in the Church, then this was a citizen of utmost value and trust. It was like that.

Rui, like Artur, compared the clandestine militant to a martyr–hero: that is, to someone who sacrifices his or her life for a greater cause. Such a comparison was based not only on his perception of the lives of others, which might be understood from the short dialogue quoted above, but on his own experiences. He was arrested along with his wife and baby by the political police and was tortured. However, he did not mention this in our conversation; and when I asked if I could interview his wife, he begged me not to as she becomes very distressed when thinking about the past. Nevertheless, some of Rui's former comrades cited his arrest and torture as an example of the cruelty of the political police, and of someone who suffered terribly at their hands. Therefore, the I-position *My comrades as martyr–heroes* was a very important pillar of trust for the interviewed militants. They knew that they were not alone in being prepared to sacrifice their lives – the risk and hardship were integral parts of a shared experience. Thus, this I-position generated strong affection and meant that conflict was almost totally eliminated within the organisation. However, it is important to note that the contextual factors in which pre-revolution militants acted, especially ARA and BR militants who were based in Portugal, were key to the absence of conflict in those organisations. The repressive political context precluded extensive interpersonal contact, which contributed to a sharp focus on the actions and goals to be accomplished, while sidelining power struggles and interpersonal rivalries. The same could not be said of LUAR militants, who moved much more freely in exile and experienced far more internal conflict, or of counter- and post-revolution militants, as we shall see later.

Pre-revolution militants: gender

As the armed wing of the PCP, the ARA followed the party's directions in the majority of issues, including gender dynamics within the organisation. The PCP presupposed that men should be involved directly in the struggle, while women should act as housewives, lending an air of normality to a difficult situation. The ARA's members justified this division of roles essentially on the basis of women's traditional cultural position in conservative Portuguese society at the time, which was *Women as housewives*. Rita, the only female former member of the ARA interviewed, was the first to acknowledge that it was difficult for a woman to move around at the time: "Men could move around better. We have to situate things at that time. In the '60s and '70s women did not have, as they do now, freedom to do whatever they wished". In this sense, Artur recognised that the PCP's meso-political narrative regarding gender had been unable to follow the party's intention of being "in the vanguard"; instead, it had followed the regime's macro-political narrative. Nevertheless, the role of women was highly valued by the ARA's militants. Artur affirmed that there was "very great pressure on women", particularly when it came to raising children and maintaining the appearance of a normal family, living a normal life, to avoid suspicion. As an example, he mentioned an episode with a neighbour in which Rita played a key role:

> She [Rita] had a specific task, which was to keep the house safe by maintaining a good relationship with the neighbourhood. [This] had to be very limited in order not to arouse suspicion, but enough to see if the neighbours had any idea about our situation. For example, we had a neighbour who liked us very much, because every day when coming home from work – she was a teacher and a great admirer of "Saint Salazar" – she would always bring a little present for our daughter, who was two or three years old. Sometimes we invited her to come in and have a little chat.
>
> [Several months later], while having lunch with our daughter, who was now about four years old, an extraordinarily interesting image appeared on the television: my face – "Wanted Terrorist" – and [pictures of] three or four other people … We were a bit stunned but our daughter did not notice anything, because I looked very different: it was a picture from the time when I was at university, with a plump face and no glasses. On that day, my wife went to the neighbour's house to ask for some parsley … [and] to see her reaction. And she had a reaction! She told her: "Did you see the terrorists on the news? One is a worker who wants to be a minister, another is a shoemaker, and one is a student who has been deceived". That was me!
>
> Rita looked clueless and said: "Well, I don't know, perhaps …"
>
> "Oh, you don't know about this?"
>
> "We don't care much about these things," and that was that for that day.

Thus, women in the ARA were seen as effective members of the organisation, albeit with a role that was different from that of the men. They were never directly involved in the commission of violent actions, but they participated in a variety of other activities, such as field research (e.g., looking for possible targets), writing articles for clandestine publications, and, most important of all, maintaining the so-called "theatre of normal life". Lídia from the BR used this expression in a contemptuous tone to describe female militancy in the ARA. In her opinion, women in the ARA could not be compared to women in the BR, because the former followed societal and PCP conventions, while the latter represented women's emancipation by assuming the same roles as men. Her point that a "qualitative leap" occurred in relation to women's role in armed organisations from the ARA to the BR is quite valid. However, women in the ARA felt they were full members of the organisation, because they shared the men's sense of agency by agreeing to engage in the political struggle. They put their lives on the line, just as the men did, and they took care of some aspects of life underground to a greater extent than the men (e.g., relationships with neighbours).

The role of women within the LUAR was not too different from what has been described within the ARA. However, the LUAR militants tended to mention only one woman – Helena Vidal – who seemingly played a pivotal role in the organisation but passed away before I conducted my fieldwork. Hence, I was unable to interview any women from the LUAR. However, within this organisation, it seems that women achieved equal respect and acknowledgement, as can be seen in Henrique's answer when I asked if there were any women in the LUAR: "There were no women in the LUAR … There were people". He then made some interesting points in relation to women's participation in the LUAR, echoing what other researchers have found when interviewing militants from other armed organisations. First, he considered that "as there were far fewer women than men, those who were willing to join and gave proof of being as operational as any man … were considered maybe more than a man who had the same attitude". This notion resonates with some of the labels presented by Brigitte Nacos (2008, p. 265), who suggests that women in armed organisations are often considered not only "tough-as-males", but "tougher-than-men". Second, despite insisting that "there was no distinction" between women and men, Henrique acknowledged that

> sometimes they did things that a man could not do. For example, when we assaulted the TAP plane in Morocco, we needed to smuggle the weapons in and Helena did it, because she pretended to be pregnant. I could not pretend to be pregnant … There are things that … a woman can do with much more success than a man. If nothing else, they can resort to seduction and … many other things that a man can't do.

Thus, for Henrique, the difference between a man and woman was the same as the difference "between two guns. You have two guns and you will choose the one that is most appropriate for the operation". The only risk of holding such an instrumental view on gender relates to the concerns of Laura Sjoberg and Caron Gentry (2007) regarding apparently positive descriptions of women's roles within armed organisations, which can mask a dynamic of using women to implement men's tactics. I do not believe that this was the situation within the LUAR. However, as already mentioned, there were very few women in the organisation, which meant their male counterparts had little or no understanding of what women's militancy was or could have been.

One pre-revolution organisation was distinguished by the fact that it recruited a large number of women who then played prominent roles in its activities: the BR. One of them was even involved in the BR's foundation and helped to direct its operations. Hence, it should come as no surprise that three of the five BR militants I interviewed were women. These interviewees offered explanations for the composition of the BR that were related to meso-political narratives based on liberationist, egalitarian, and emancipatory stances. This organisation wanted its women to be symbols of social equality and transformation and to serve as examples for other women. Thus, Adriano, one of the BR's co-founders, believed that,

> from a political perspective, it was essential for us to present ourselves with women, because there was a part of the population who just seeing men would not feel drawn to the activity. Women would not feel attracted to the activity.

Specifically to highlight the organisation's gender views, one BR militant wore a miniskirt during a bank robbery. Of course, such garments were frowned upon in what was still a deeply conservative country during the dictatorship. Adriano aimed

> to show women who wore miniskirts that there were other ways to express themselves, that there were girls in miniskirts who had the audacity to do that sort of thing. So, it was a way of communicating a message in conditions of censorship.

In this sense, he recognised that the BR "always had a policy, sometimes a little bit artificial, of bringing women into the armed struggle process". This was related to the BR's meso-political narratives regarding gender issues, but also to the belief that women

> are less prone to violence, to gratuitous violence, and are more resilient, because they were in a dominated situation for many centuries. Consequently, they know how to resist. They have psychological resources that seemed interesting from the point of view of armed action.

Adriano's views on the importance of ensuring a visible female presence during armed actions echoes Leila Khaled's[1] response when she was asked why she was chosen by the Popular Front for the Liberation of Palestine (PFLP) to carry out several high-profile missions: "They had wanted a woman to show to the world that women were involved in the revolution" (MacDonald, 1991, p. 108). The BR wanted to fight sexism and liberate women from the domination and oppression they had suffered for centuries. In other words, one of the organisation's goals was societal transformation, which was similar to the perspective of a former ETA commando interviewed by Eileen MacDonald (1991, p. 21): "ETA is the vanguard of our revolution. If the revolution plans to change society, it means that the vanguard has to change its own attitudes towards women in the first place". Finally, Adriano insisted that women are less violent and more resilient than men – a recurring theme in MacDonald's interviews with various women who have been involved in political violence. In this context, we are again confronted with the fine line between women's emancipation through participation in the armed struggle and women's subjugation through serving men's purposes in that same struggle. However, in our conversations, the former BR women declared that they never felt that they were treated differently from the men. Above all, they insisted that they were all people, militants, and comrades, not women.

Counter-revolution militants: escaping into exile

Going underground for militants who belonged to the ELP and the MDLP took a different form in comparison to the cases of the pre-revolution militants described above. A core group of counter-revolution militants chose to escape from Portugal either immediately after 25 April 1974 or after 11 March 1975 (see Chapter 1 for more information on the events that took place on these dates). Spain was undoubtedly the first choice for all of these fugitives due to its geographical proximity, but also because it offered them a warm welcome. This concentration of exiles, who not only supported the deposed regime but declared their opposition to leftism, helped to swell the ranks of the emergent counter-revolutionary movements. According to Ilídio from the MDLP, this allowed them to take their "revenge" against the "hated communists, who made them run away from their homes". Various interviewees shared his impression that Spain sympathised with the Portuguese counter-revolutionary movements, on account of the fact that it granted political asylum to those who requested it and did not pester those who did not, leaving them free to carry on with their affairs. According to Ilídio, "the Spanish authorities often turned a blind eye" to his organisation's political activities. In this sense, counter-revolution militants who were based in Spain experienced life underground only when travelling back to Portugal, where they often faced charges relating to army desertion and counter-insurgency. Nevertheless, a few counter-revolution militants never left Portugal and were considered clandestine by their own organisations. However, Ilídio assumed that life underground was not too complicated for such militants: "Those who were inside did not have problems. They were clandestine, but they could move around with open doors because no one knew who they were".

Thus, the police's pursuit of counter-revolution militants was not as severe as its persecution of pre-revolution militants, who had the authorities constantly at their heels and needed to exercise extreme caution to avoid detection. This speaks to the turbulent political context of the so-called PREC (*Processo Revolucionário em Curso* / Ongoing Revolutionary Process), which prevailed between 25 April 1974 and 25 November 1975. During this period, the country was divided between the conservative north and the liberal south, with both sides becoming more extremist and driving the country towards civil war. In this context, both the ELP and the MDLP were able to find safe havens not only in Spain (albeit less so as time went by), but also among the fervent Portuguese Catholic Church and the people of northern Portugal. This resulted in two zones where counter-revolution militants could move around with ease – one in neighbouring Spain and the other within Portugal, north of the Douro.

Counter-revolution militants: challenges

The challenges of underground life for counter-revolution militants were mainly related to interpersonal dynamics, and especially to the power relations that are peculiar to the military. In this sense, Sérgio explained that military people

> have a spirit of unity when there is a very clear mission, with very clear borders. When the mission is more wide-ranging, military people are like women, if you'll pardon the expression. They are terrible, because they organise into small cliques and groups and little leaders.

Thus, according to Sérgio, being a member of the MDLP posed a number of challenges for a few military people who were used to undertaking specific missions and knowing their place in a fixed chain of command. In the context of a looser organisation, they tended to focus on power issues to the detriment of achieving the MDLP's goals. This was what led Sérgio to draw the clearly derogatory parallel between ex-military militants and women (and thereby reflect the sexism that continues to permeate Portuguese society).

Other MDLP militants mentioned challenges regarding the contrasting roles of operational militants (i.e., those who executed the actions) and ideologues (i.e., those who planned the actions). According to Ilídio, some members of the organisation were much more comfortable with the latter role: "terrific thinkers, but if we told them to do something, they started shaking". Meanwhile, others were well equipped to act: "essentially operational militants. It was not worth telling them: 'Think!' With an operational you would say, 'Do this!' and they would know how to do it". Ilídio added that a good leader would know how to get the most out of the various militants and deploy their respective skills to the greatest advantage.

The former members of counter-revolution organisations were the only ones to mention important external relationships. This differentiated them from both pre- and post-revolution organisations, which were much more isolated. In this sense, a number of militants affirmed that they maintained contact with important political figures in Portugal, including the prime minister and the president. They would discuss crucial issues with these high-ranking politicians, especially the apparent imminence of a civil war. However, it is important to bear in mind that this meso-level difference between counter-revolution and pre- and post-revolution militants was due to the fact that some of the former had been important figures within the regime (e.g., General Spínola, the leader of the MDLP, was the country's first president after the April Revolution). Hence, they were in a much stronger position to maintain external contacts and relations. In addition, the MDLP had privileged relations with the secret services of other countries through its Information Bureau. The man responsible for this bureau explained that a number of foreign secret services, including those of the United States and France, were especially interested in information on people who were boarding planes from Portugal to the Eastern Bloc.

Thus, according to counter-revolution militants, most of the challenges they faced underground related to the management of interpersonal relations, both within and outside the organisation. Within the organisation, power relations that mirrored hierarchical arrangements and differences between ideologues and operational militants caused stressful situations and could lead militants to question their loyalty to the organisation. However, unlike clandestine militants in general, counter-revolution militants did not burn their bridges with important mainstream political figures. On the contrary, they persevered in trying to influence Portuguese political life and achieve their goals through negotiation, which may have contributed to an easier return to normal life in Portugal after the dissolution of the organisation (see Chapter 5 for more details).

Counter-revolution militants: gender

There were very few women in counter-revolution organisations. According to the accounts of the men who were interviewed for this study, those who did enlist played a very secondary role. For instance, Daniel from the MDLP only vaguely remembered one or two women in the Political Analysis Bureau. However, in his opinion, they did not have any “political importance”, because the MDLP “was a structure of men”. Dinis expanded on this perspective when he explained that excluding women from the organisation spared them from trouble. In much the same way as pre-revolution militants, he located his organisation’s gender dynamics firmly within the context of 1970s Portugal, where the dominant cultural position was *Women as housewives*:

> You need to see that in 1975 we did not talk much about the emancipation of women. There was more the concept of the woman as a housewife who would guarantee the children’s upbringing. There were very few women working. That’s how it was in the ’70s.

However, the scarcity and secondary role of women among counter-revolution organisations mirrored not only the macro-cultural position of the time, but also meso-political narratives. Counter-revolution organisations were mainly composed of ex-military people – militants who were recruited from institutions that counted very small numbers of women among their ranks (see Torrão, 2008). This gave rise to meso-political narratives regarding the need to spare women from any task other than looking after the house and the children. Nevertheless, this is no excuse for portraying women, in general, in a pejorative, stereotypical manner, as several counter-revolution interviewees did. One example is the parallel Sérgio drew between leaderless military men and women, which implied that women tend to form cliques specifically to undermine and fight each other. Another example is Ilídio’s comment that “there were some wives of some people who were linked to the movement, who thought that one glass was more important than another. You see, these normal intrigues”. Such examples provide a window into counter-revolution militants' opinions of women in the 1970s, and in some cases these seem to have changed little over time.

Post-revolution militants: going underground

Various FP-25 militants described their experiences of going underground. A few remembered the precise moment when they severed all contact with family and friends and adopted a new identity. These memories were quite similar to those of pre-revolution militants. Mariana, who spent six years living underground, believed that she "must have been the one who lived underground the longest". At first, she coped well with the choice she had made. However, over time, she found it increasingly difficult:

> I had immense needs. The family had stayed behind, I had no contact with the family. What cost me most, in fact, was that I could not do a number of things that I wanted to do. I once had to flee the theatre halfway through because the police entered. If I'd go to a café, I had to be watchful of those who came and left, because we had to leave if the police came, and that happened countless times.

Yet, most of the FP-25 interviewees described a "lighter", less cautious, and more "mixed" situation that imposed less of a financial and logistical burden on the organisation's structure. Hélder explained that this was due to the fact that the clandestine movement was composed of human beings who followed similar patterns of behaviour to the rest of human society:

> The clandestine movement was a society like a normal society. We are made of flesh and blood, we have our frustrations and joys, we have our passions, we have a desire to fulfil our dreams ... Children are raised, some comrades even had children in jail, because conditions were created for this.

Clearly, Hélder felt the need to highlight the humanity of politically violent militants, giving voice to the position *We as human beings*. And, as human beings – rather than programmed, violent automata – militants had needs and feelings and found it hard to abandon their previous lives completely. For instance, Bruno confided that, while he found clandestine life very strenuous, he enjoyed occasional moments of recreation:

> I happened to be a guy who never refrained ... I am known as an underground dude who went to discos at night and all ... I was very fond of African music and dancing ... I had a lot of fun.

However, he recognised that he was far from typical and acknowledged that he was able to behave in this way only because he had a large support network.

Júlia joined the FP-25 in 1980 but did not always live underground before her arrest in 1985. This was mainly due to the need to fulfil her role as a mother. Her first child was born around the time she first engaged with the FP-25. Her second was born when she was a committed militant: "My second son was born and I gave him my own surname at the clinic where he was born, but in a very hasty fashion". Later, she fell pregnant again, and her third child was born in prison. Thus, she felt she was always "in a more or less safeguarded position", which meant "moving house almost every month" and "weaving around to prevent being identified".

Júlia's account of the early part of her life within the organisation reflected the core position *I as a committed militant*. Moreover, her narrative also suggested the existence of other pro-commitment centripetal I-positions that not only seemed congruent with but also fed her core position. One of these was *I as a loyal comrade*, which might have strengthened her identification with and commitment to the organisation's goals, even in times of great difficulty and disagreement, when she remembered thinking: "We're all in this, I won't simply turn my back". This loyalty was perceived as reciprocal, and Júlia freely acknowledged her reliance on other members of the organisation: "I wasn't alone. There were people in whom I trusted. I think that was key". However, her dominant political position – *I as a fully committed FP-25 militant* – was difficult to reconcile with other positions that could inhibit her involvement with the organisation. One of these was *I as a mother*, which was subjugated by her organisational relationships and the political struggle. Thus, her children lived intermittently with Júlia's parents or moved around with her. Another subjugated I-position, in this context, was *I as a partner*. Júlia believed that her engagement with the struggle prevented the establishment of intimate, stable relationships: "This was related to the type of political choices I made. These choices held a key place in my thinking and thus the idea of having a partner didn't really have any bearing". This detachment from family ties and stable, intimate relationships was reinforced by the living conditions underground, which limited her options and intensified her identification with the organisation's collective identity: "Because, after a certain point, you can't go back … You can't re-enter the legal structure. You can't simply go home". Both the dominance of Júlia's *I as a loyal comrade* position and the subjugation of her family-related positions, such as *I as a mother*, are clear signs of affective closure. For Júlia, being a loyal comrade was the aspect of her militancy that kept her going. She felt that she had to be there for her comrades, as they were present for her. This type of closure, her narrative suggested, inhibited her ability to imagine other life scenarios, fuelling the perception that her sole option was to remain fully committed to her militant identity.

In this vein, the depth of the clandestine experience seemed to vary among the FP-25 militants. Some dived deep underground from the outset, while others tried to maintain a degree of connection with their previous lives above ground. However, the latter was an option for only a limited period of time, because arrests and police harassment inevitably increased the sense of being a full-time clandestine militant. Moreover, as Júlia mentioned, there was a culture of no going back. Militants could not simply tire of the organisation or the struggle and decide to leave, because they had nowhere else to go. Hence, their options were: keep going; die during a confrontation with the police; face imprisonment; or flee to a foreign country. All of these options will be explored in depth in Chapter 5.

Post-revolution militants: challenges

The accounts of post-revolution militants about the challenges of underground life mainly related to interpersonal conflicts caused by stressful daily routines. House sharing, for instance, was frequently cited as one of the most challenging issues. Júlia reported that militants were usually not allowed to choose their housemates. Instead, these were selected by the leadership, who focused on assembling teams to execute future missions and other logistical matters (e.g., a shortage of funds to rent another house) rather than personal issues. As a result, people who had never met one another were often thrown together, which could lead to good or terrible relationships. Júlia experienced

> a little bit of everything: people with whom I avoided speaking; people with whom it was very difficult to discuss what we would eat the next day; but also people with whom I shared a relationship for life. But it was fractious, in general. It was tense because we were always short of money, and there was always great tension regarding whether the house was safe or not. People had to behave so that we did not have to leave the next day… In that sense, the situation was not very comfortable.

These conflictual relationships were clearly rooted in the context in which militants were living. This was characterised by a stressful daily routine, not only because people did not know one another well and each person had their own views and patterns of behaviour, but also because their living conditions made life difficult. Here, many of the interviewees cited the organisation's lack of money and poor logistics. Indeed, Mariana reported that she sometimes starved because she had insufficient funds to buy food. And Júlia suggested that the "dominant feeling" of her whole underground experience was related to the stress of daily life due to the shortage of money and poor logistics:

> There was a permanent lack of money, bad cars, weapons that did not work, very rudimentary logistics, very badly suited to what we wanted to do. We were always amending situations; we were always looking for money to take care of the essentials.

In this sense, the material aspects of underground life had a detrimental effect on post-revolution militants' experiences and added significant layers of stress to their involvement with a politically violent organisation, influencing the ways in which they related to each other and prompting interpersonal conflict. Little by little, these circumstances started to gain a voice and, as I shall explore further in Chapter 5, encouraged the disengagement-prone position *My organisation is inefficient and unprepared.*

At the individual level, several militants felt that life underground presented many psychological challenges. They felt that they were living in an environment that made them prone to "seeing ghosts", because they were constantly on guard and always suspected everyone around them. This state of mind was accompanied by high levels of stress and fatigue that were never assuaged. As we have seen, Hélder termed these challenges a "huge psychological game" and believed that clandestine militants needed extraordinary reserves of self-control to deal with the "shadows" and "noises" of daily life and maintain "psychological balance". Otherwise, they would sit by the window, noting down the number plates of passing cars in order to convince themselves that they were not being watched and the safe house was still safe. In this sense, as Hélder and other interviewees articulated, clandestine militants needed to devise strategies to deal with "psychological games". For Hélder, this was as simple as following the guidelines in the "underground manuals or even the novelists' literature": for instance, never turn your back to the door when eating at a restaurant. Meanwhile, Jaime would walk two or three times around the neighbourhood before going home to ensure that he had not been followed. Such strategies could bring some peace of mind to the militants and helped them achieve the much-needed "psychological balance". Nevertheless, Hélder recalled that some of his comrades still wilted under the pressure because they lacked "inner strength and conviction". Moreover, there were consequences even for those who played the game right to the end, including Hélder himself: "You get to a point when you step into a double personality and you do not easily extricate yourself from that. Even today I still have some things, habits that I still have".

Finally, a few militants viewed the closed and fragmented nature of clandestine organisations as an obstacle to achieving their goals. Organisations such as the FP-25 are usually compartmentalised into small cells that undertake individual missions. They are also characterised by a lack of debate among the whole membership, a measure that is designed to protect the organisation and its militants from exposure and arrest. Therefore, militants often focus on daily matters relating to their personal survival and safety, rather than the bigger picture, as Júlia explained:

> The fact that the organisation is completely clandestine creates great limitations. People shut themselves within a world that is very centred on small goals, particularly the objectives of each operation … so there is little communication with the rest of society. Therefore, this creates great difficulties for relaxed daily living. The organisation, by imposing its political choices, was a violent organisation, clandestine, and consequently very

fragmented, which greatly limited the ability of people to discuss the decisions.

This detachment from society and the militants' increasing dependence on the organisation contributed to the process of cognitive closure. Through this process, militants' perceptions of the world outside the organisation were deeply transformed. Furthermore, this process contributed to the maintenance of the core position *I as a committed militant*, on which the functioning of other I-positions depended. This sheds light on why militants maintain long-term commitment to clandestine organisations, despite all of the daily hardships and emotional hurdles. In a sense, their lives become encrusted in an indisputable self-narrative in which they are categorised as committed militants and trusted comrades, who are personally responsible for the survival of the organisation. In this context, they feel that very little needs to be discussed, but much needs to be done to keep the organisation afloat.

Post-revolution militants: gender

Within the FP-25, very few women were directly involved with armed actions. Nine women were eventually imprisoned, compared with roughly sixty men. Only four of the nine had ever lived underground. The other five were supporters of the organisation or had fulfilled logistical roles (e.g., sheltering militants, hiding weapons and ammunition). Jaime found this under-representation of women deplorable. However, he felt that the few active women within the FP-25 were "the same as the men". Hélder agreed, although he remembered that some of the older militants did not agree with the women's participation in violent missions. Júlia stated bluntly that the FP-25 was "deeply sexist" and continued: "everything was done in a logic of manliness and virility … not virility in the strictly sexual sense, but in the affirmation of strength and courage". She felt frustrated by the prevalence of such sexist attitudes within a leftist organisation, because she believed that these were "concepts that maybe the left should be able to abolish". In this context, she lamented that none of the four women of the FP-25 was able to make a significant mark on the organisation. In her opinion, she and the other women "voted, participated in discussions … but whether it was these four women or another set of four women would not have changed the reality of the organisation". Thus, once more, macro-level cultural positions influenced the meso- and micro-level gender dynamics within an armed organisation, since a number of FP-25's men were still bound by social prejudice and tradition relating to women and to what it was to be a man.

Júlia also mentioned that the organisation's attitude towards women in terms of romantic relationships mirrored the prevailing sexist tradition. For instance, she implied that the female members were expected to sleep with the men: "Despite the discourse of vanguard – 'We are all equal, we are all equal' – they did not sleep with each other. When they looked for someone to sleep with, they looked for women". In Júlia's opinion, this was detrimental to the women's emotional well-being: "The emotional side of people who were underground was not very healthy. The few women never lacked company. I don't know if this equated to settled affection. Generally, I don't think so". However, she acknowledged that it was hard to avoid such situations, echoing Hélder's *We as human beings* position. People have affective needs within a circumscribed universe, as Júlia explained:

> Almost all [of the female militants] got involved with people who were in the organisation, but I think that was inevitable, because our universe was quite limited. It was not very easy to find a boyfriend around the corner, because we did not go to clubs and stuff. There was a world completely closed to us and this was the universe people had got into.

Despite suffering the pernicious influence of macro-level sexist attitudes within the organisation, in another way FP-25 actually benefited from the prevailing *Portuguese society as utterly sexist* position. The police would "never see a woman as a potential enemy", as Hélder explained. And Júlia remembered several occasions when she thought she was sure to be caught, but she escaped because the police officers "were always looking for men, even though they knew there were women" in the organisation.

The use of violence

I feel it is important to include a section on the use of violence because this topic emerged repeatedly when former militants recounted their stories. All of the interviewees were aware that it was not my intention to gather detailed information about specific actions, such as who did what, where, and how. Rather, I was interested in hearing first-hand accounts of their personal experiences, emotions, and thoughts in relation to the commission of politically violent acts. Thus, in this section, I will explore former militants' accounts of the armed actions that their organisations undertook. I will particularly focus on the I-positions enacted by various militants regarding the commission of violence, but will also explore their perceptions of the sources and dynamics of popular support for their organisations' causes.

Pre-revolution militants: armed actions

Despite offering conceptual justifications for armed action, a number of pre-revolution militants displayed personal distaste for guns and explosives. A few of them insisted that it was "not in their nature" to use guns, which they did only as a last resort. Henrique from the LUAR, for instance, considered that "the best armed struggle tactic is to disarm the struggle". His organisation, as well as the ARA and the BR, pursued a strong and clear "no kill" policy.

Henrique believed that he could not "simultaneously fight for freedom and be the destroyer of someone's life". Additionally, he considered that "the problem was social and political", so it could not be solved by taking the life of a single tyrant. Thus, pre-revolution militants argued that human targets would only weaken the political struggle, reduce their popular support, and allow the regime to label them "terrorists" or treat them as common criminals.

When asked about their feelings towards the commission of violent actions, a handful of pre-revolution militants admitted to feeling afraid. However, as Henrique explained, they tended to view the I-position *I as someone who is afraid* in a positive light. By contrast, he believed that over-confidence was far more dangerous:

> Fear always. May God deliver us from those who are not afraid. I met some who were not afraid because they were confident. Fear always. Courage is not lack of fear. Courage is to do what you have to do while being very afraid.

Some pre-revolution militants also mentioned their fear of arrest and torture by the political police. As Leonel from the ARA said: "I was not afraid of death. I was afraid of suffering, being imprisoned and tortured".

Thus, these militants had to devise strategies to deal with the emotional turmoil that inevitably preceded each mission. Henrique recalled:

> When I was little, I had a difficult life … [but] each of us has his ghosts … My biggest dream, when I was growing up, was to have a bath – a tub so I could take a warm bath. That was my biggest dream … [So], before each action, I always tried to find a way to take a good bath and I would say: "This one is done. Nobody can take this one away from me, right? From here on, no matter what happens …" We always have mechanisms, we always find mechanisms; but whatever mechanism we have, there is a certain time after which we don't care about what might happen. When I say we don't care about what might happen I mean that there is a point after which we no longer think about it. It's been thought out and decided that we have to do this and that, and that's that. So, let's get on with it. There is nothing else we can do.

Superficially, it seems farcical that Henrique tried to take a warm bath before each mission. However, on deeper reflection, it is apparent that the bath served as a means for him to deal with the internal chaos that preceded each action: some of his I-positions would have voiced the fear of being killed or arrested; others would have emphasised the risk that is involved in achieving socio-political transformation; and still others would have articulated the despair of separation from loved ones and the yearning for a regular life. In this context, Henrique's warm bath brought balance to these divergent I-positions. It allowed him to enjoy the realisation of a childhood dream and helped him to focus on what had to be done.

At the end of his account, Henrique displayed a level of commitment that was shared by almost every other militant: the unshakeable conviction that the planned action must be carried out, irrespective of what might happen. Thus, a number of militants described experiencing a sense of calm immediately before an action. However, they tended to feel very different later, as Adriano from the BR explained: "I was never afraid or stressed before an action. I never questioned its execution, nor thought about going back. The stress would come afterwards. Then I used to throw up, suffer diarrhoea and insomnia, but always *after* the mission".

Several of the militants described the day of an action as "joyful", because it was "a day of celebration for the revolutionary". As Henrique explained, each mission was the culmination of considerable hardship, but the act itself was rarely mentioned in the build-up, despite its obvious importance. He echoed feelings expressed by several other interviewees from all three pre-revolution organisations regarding the daily routine of a full-time militant. Their lives were usually a depressing combination of stress, frustration, and disappointment due to precarious living conditions, a lack of resources, and the death or arrest of comrades. It was only on action days that they experienced any sort of joy, but that was sufficient to carry them through the dark days of life underground, at least for a time. Yet, the gap between the imagined identity of the clandestine militant, who had all the resources he or she needed to pursue socio-political transformation, and what was actually happening in everyday life, became, little by little, increasingly difficult to ignore.

Pre-revolution militants: popular support

The pre-revolution militants' attitudes towards armed actions were guided by a strong desire to garner popular support and approval. These militants did not want to fight for their own benefit. They aimed to win people's hearts and minds in order to attain socio-political transformation for everyone. Thus, in the context of the use of violence, they displayed the I-position *I as part of a non-terrorist organisation which does not kill people*. This position worked both to justify their violent actions against the structures of the state, rather than people, and to generate support among non-militants. Such support (be it real or imagined) fed engagement-prone I-positions that subjugated other valued voices. As Henrique emphatically explained, violent action makes sense only when it represents the will of the people:

> If the revolutionary is a fish, people are the water. Fish do not live without water. So, when you are preparing your arm, be it to punch or to shoot, your arm has to be an extension of many arms that would like to do the same thing.

Hence, Henrique believed that he assumed responsibility for being the arm that fought on behalf of all the other arms, and sacrificed his personal contact with his children to improve the lives of all the children (see Chapter 3). However, an important question should be raised here: how did the pre-revolution organisations measure their popular support? Various militants admitted that this was no easy task, especially when they were living in exile or underground for security reasons. Nevertheless, they described some methods. For instance, after an action, non-clandestine militants could gauge people's reactions by eavesdropping on conversations at their places of work, on the street, in cafés, or on public transport. Some BR militants also insisted that most people displayed no fear of them during bank robberies, because they knew that the organisation's aims were political and that it would not use violence against members of the public. Indeed, one former militant remembered receiving a round of applause during a bank raid from some people standing on the street outside. That said, on another occasion, a number of angry citizens followed the militants and were only dispersed after some shots were fired into the air. Hence, the pre-revolution militants' perceptions of popular support were quite subjective and certainly event-specific. Nevertheless, they helped to bolster engagement-prone I-positions.

Counter-revolution militants: armed actions

The armed actions of counter-revolution militants targeted the PCP. According to Afonso, the ELP

> especially encouraged uprisings of the population in the various villages, towns and cities against the headquarters of the Communist Party. When there were markets and fairs, we took advantage and carried out armed break-ins, destroying the premises, papers, and so on.

However, he added a very important detail: an I-position concerning the use of violence – *I as part of a Catholic organisation which does not commit gratuitous violence.*

> As we have a Christian background, and we are not Marxists, the guideline that always existed in this organisation was: the ends do not justify the means. We cannot begin to have gratuitous violence, but we must have clear objectives to give the people the strength and confidence to rebel.

To illustrate this I-position, Afonso recalled an occasion during his militancy when he had an opportunity to plant a bomb at a major PCP event which would be attended by all of the party's national hierarchy, as well as guests from international communist parties. He was tempted to do it – and kill maybe 90 per cent of the attendees – because he viewed the PCP as "the enemy":

> In those days, we felt we had the right to react. I mean, who was more of an enemy? Was it the FRELIMO, the MPLA I fought in the bush in Angola and Mozambique, or these PCP guys who were doing everything to destroy the rest of Portugal? For me, as a military man, they were the enemy.

Moreover, he was certain that a communist would not have hesitated if the roles had been reversed: "If I had had a communist's training, I would have said 'yes', right?" However, the *I as part of a Catholic organisation which does not commit gratuitous violence* I-position spoke louder. For Afonso, this served as proof that his struggle was fundamentally different from the struggle of leftist factions:

> That's the big distinction between a movement like the ELP and a terrorist movement, the communist guerrillas we know throughout the world. The members of the ELP had a Christian background, which obliged them to consider the use of violence very carefully.

He felt that the ELP was an organisation that adhered to higher principles and acted in defence of a righteous cause, which led to the conclusion that his obligations were fulfilled. Hence, his conscience remained clear: "I am glad to have been able to do what I did, both in the military and afterwards. I even take a certain pride in it".

The MDLP militants' attitudes towards the killings that occurred during their period of militancy were far from clear-cut. Ilídio asserted that "there was a great concern not to kill" throughout the MDLP, and, interestingly, then employed exactly the same metaphor that Henrique from the LUAR introduced earlier: "It is the famous maxim of Mao Zedong: the guerrilla must live in the crowd like fish in water. If not, it becomes the enemy". Sérgio, another MDLP militant, similarly insisted that "there were no physical attacks. It can be said that we did not kill", although he admitted, "at meetings, we gave some consideration to physical attacks on people, which today makes me put my head in my hands to think that this was even discussed". Other militants felt that the organisation was directly responsible for some deaths, but they preferred not to talk about the subject.

Thus, in terms of the use of violence by the MDLP, and particularly assassinations, the circumstances were not clearly defined by the participants in this study. Some of them sought to absolve the organisation of any responsibility for violent action, while others were prepared to point the finger at the MDLP and, specifically, at some of their former comrades. Eduardo Dâmaso (1997, p. 12) encountered similar mixed messages and interpreted the militants' testimonies as proof that intra-organisation relationships tend to be rather fragile: "in the overwhelming majority of cases the only things that lasted were hatred, resentment, serious allegations, insinuations, defamations, accusations, leaving in the air a perfume of total distrust about the true role played by various individuals". In this context, it is worth noting that most counter-revolution militants (as well as most pre- and post-revolution militants) display a range of identity positions in support of their version of events, which they defend as representative of what actually happened. Such I-positions are at the service of the construction of their sense of self and identity. They also ensure continuity between the past and the present, and allow former militants' positioning for the future.

Counter-revolution militants: popular support

Counter-revolution militants perceived that the people of the north of Portugal and the Catholic Church were strong and steadfast supporters of their cause. The reasons for this perception were linked to the cultural positions ingrained in their own identity systems. The support of the northerners was explained by their lack of support for communism, because, as Dinis suggested, they "did not want to see their land devastated". It was different in the rest of the country, because, according to Dinis, the population was coerced by the PCP: "In Lisbon and in the Alentejo, it was difficult to raise a voice and to oppose. After all, fear and coercion were dominant". Meanwhile, the support of the Catholic Church was connected to the fact that this was still the "Church that comes from the old regime", as Sérgio explained. Ilídio added that that this was a Church which, if necessary, would "bring a popular army to arms" to fight the "red invasion".

Other militants mentioned that they enjoyed the support of considerable proportions of the military and the police. This support allowed them to cross the border between Spain and Portugal with ease. However, while a number of militants passionately attested that their cause enjoyed robust popular support, Daniel held a different perspective:

> There is a fantastic book by a great Spanish writer from the time of the Carlist Wars,[2] which I read when I was in Spain and which made me laugh because it was exactly what was happening to us. It was about the immigrants in France, who thought that the country was eager for their return, that the country was waiting with open arms to welcome them, saying: "We need you to come". It was not true. The country continued to live normally. So, did I ever know if we had support? I had no idea at all. Those who wandered in and out talked about enormous popular support, but in the Carlist Wars, in Algiers, Delgado … they all said the same. Whenever there is a force that wants to overthrow a regime or wants to fight abuse of a system, there is also self-intoxication – people believe that the country is waiting for them. Probably, just as the country was not communist, it was not MDLP either. It wasn't anything. It just wanted to be left alone. That's what I think, but I cannot be sure.

This was a very different – and unusually balanced – perspective on the intensity of the MDLP's popular support. While both the north's and the

Catholic Church's support for these militants' cause has been well documented (see, e.g., Dâmaso, 1997; Hortelão, Baêna and Sousa, 2012; Carvalho, 2017), maybe it was not *all* of the north or *all* of the Catholic Church. Maybe the north and the Catholic Church responded in different ways to different types of commitment requested by armed organisations (even if, in principle, they agreed with their cause). Maybe those Portuguese who were not communist were also reluctant to join a civil war on the side of counter-revolution militants. Daniel's testimony introduces all of these interesting "maybes". He has clearly constructed them over the course of many years of internal and external dialogue, but, at the same time, has resisted the temptation to romanticise and inflate the importance and role of his former organisation. This seems to be a consequence of his dominant I-positions regarding his past militancy. He considered that his militancy was motivated by the I-position *I as a young idealist*, which was justified and supported by his young age, which made him feel responsible for the fate of his country and to believe that he could be of service. Today, Daniel presents a clear cut in his identity system regarding the past. It is acknowledged, justified, and performed according to his present positions, including a successful career outside politics, which grants him the status of a public figure in Portuguese society.

Post-revolution militants: armed actions

Some FP-25 militants, such as Jaime, felt that the organisation's armed actions acted as a brake against exploitative employers. In a context where "the state did not act", Jaime believed that "shooting the knee" of an abusive employer would "convey a practical message for both sides – for the employers and for the victims who had been laid off". Thus, the FP-25 was composed of militants who saw the need to take justice into their own hands, encouraged by a perception that the state preferred to protect the powerful rather than the vulnerable. However, opinions about the best type of violent action to perform were not as homogeneous as the goal that had brought the militants together in the first place. In fact, several militants mentioned endless discussions and conflicts about the two main options: violence that would not endanger people's lives and violence that would. The militants who considered that people should not be killed were not motivated by personal morality. Rather, they believed that such actions would be ineffective and counter-productive, as Bruno explained:

> I was against the killings, not for moral reasons, but for tactical reasons … I considered that if we wanted to lead by example, in pedagogical terms it was preferable to put them in a wheelchair, transform them into living examples. Pedagogically, that would work better than killing the guy. [An assassination] would make the news, but after a while, nobody would talk about it anymore; it would be forgotten. [But if we put him] in a wheelchair: the guy did this, but *that* happened.

On the other side of the argument, Júlia advocated killing representatives of the class that the FP-25 were fighting against – "a symbol of the employers" – to serve as an example for the workers and encourage their struggle: "I thought that this was the type of action that could trigger the workers' reaction. I mean, the fact that that person was reached could trigger a sense of strength and lead the workers to react".

Eventually, the FP-25 opted for the second option, and a number of militants justified this decision by highlighting the way in which the targeted victims were perceived. Jaime, for instance, felt that there were always socio-political reasons for the killings:

> If people – historians, or people like you – studied the FP-25 actions in which people died, you would see that there was a reason. I mean, the path of those who turned out to be victims of the attacks of the FP-25 was a path that showed that they were willing to …

Jaime did not finish this sentence. Instead, he started to list the organisation's assassination targets and offered justifications for each:

> For example, the Gelmar guy was used by the government to close companies. He would arrive and destroy the company. That was his speciality! … At Sacavém Tableware Factory, there were several suicides caused by the life the employer imposed on the workers [such as unpaid wages] … In the case of [Gaspar] Castelo Branco [General Manager of the Prison Service] there were people who fell ill: he was a tyrant, he was a *salazarista* … Doctors would say that people needed to go to hospital and he would say, "No, I am the boss here," which led doctors to resign. The prime minister did not give it any importance because he was the General Manager of the Prison Service … How should the organisation deal with the situation at that time? Send him a postcard wishing him happy holidays? In addition to his behaviour regarding the prisoners in general, what he was doing with FP-25 prisoners was totally inhuman … These are actions that I personally understand, and I understand them as messages that need to be pushed through.

For Jaime, the FP-25's victims were actually perpetrators, because they were responsible for the suffering of others. Therefore, ending their lives was not only justified but could prevent future abuse of power by conveying a message that was "as clear as water".

In addition to justifying the assassination of these targets, Jaime defended the retribution that the FP-25 meted out to so-called "penitents" – arrested militants who collaborated with the police in exchange for reduced prison sentences. According to Bruno,

> It was assumed that guys who clearly betrayed [the organisation], who chose to go to the other side and cooperate with the police, including

> joining them in searches for militants, of course, if we had the chance, we would kill those guys.

Hence, despite his general aversion towards killing, Bruno was not against the murder of penitents. This seemed to be viewed as a legitimate punishment within the organisation, and none of the FP-25 interviewees was willing to condemn it. In fact, the opposite was true, as is exemplified in Júlia's poignant testimony:

> Well, in all honesty, the day I heard on the radio "FP-25 penitent killed", I leapt for joy and said, "Hallelujah! At last" … They are not really people to me. I would not care if I saw them lying on the sidewalk, frankly.

Thus, the accounts of post-revolution militants who condoned murder were characterised by certain voices that empowered violence-prone I-positions: the voice of entitlement, the voice of betrayal, and the voice of coercion. The voice of entitlement stated that the organisation's targets were not victims but perpetrators of inhuman injustice. The voice of betrayal spoke intimately to the hearts of the militants, even those who did not agree with the policy of targeting human life in general. Finally, the voice of coercion underlined the organisation's lack of options. In that specific context, the militants felt that there was no other means to attain their goals.

The post-revolution militants expressed negative feelings towards only one of their missions, in which a baby was accidentally killed. According to the militants who were interviewed, this was the only truly innocent victim of any FP-25 action. This death had a serious impact on the organisation: the militants' ties, both among themselves and towards the organisation, were weakened, causing numerous arguments and endless finger-pointing. Bruno, for instance, felt that "it was an accident, but an accident caused by the negligence of the guys who carried it out. It was not their intention, but they did things wrong". Nevertheless, the FP-25 kept launching further missions, since the baby's death, intentional or not, was seen as an unfortunate consequence of a vital political struggle. In addition, a few of the interviewees stressed that members of the organisation were also killed in that struggle, and they found their deaths equally difficult and painful. Thus, in most cases, the I-position *I as a militant who does not regret the organisation's violent acts* remains dominant to this day. For instance, Jaime defended his perspective as follows:

> Everyone speaks about the victims. But what about the FP-25 militants who died? There weren't just one or two of them; there were several. They did not die from car accidents, right? So, I have the same respect for the "victims", shall we say, as for my comrades, because I think that the political struggle is the political struggle … So, my answer is that I am

> not sorry for anything I did. I believe that violence is a means of political struggle.

In this sense, it seems that regret positions have no place within militants' identity systems, even when there is disagreement about some of the organisation's tactics. Maybe this was why Jaime felt a need to justify his past militancy, even on his wedding day:

> This does not mean that I think or that I can say that I live well or interacted well with those decisions or situations [the assassinations]. I do not live well with anything … But it's like I said on my wedding day: this is part of the political struggle … I have as much respect for people who eventually died at the hands of the FP-25 – some by accident, others, of course, through the determination of the organisation – as I do for my comrades who also died in that fight.

Finally, some militants argued that the organisation's less political violent missions, such as bank robberies, were perceived as necessary for its survival. Júlia, for instance, suggested that she developed the I-position *I as an FP-25 militant who prioritises collective decisions over individual reasoning*, which meant that she was able to bypass normal processes of self-reflection and almost automatically justify certain violent acts: "We more or less acquired a rhythm of doing things and we weren't always thinking about if we were doing the *right* thing". Such behaviour seems to result from the centripetal movement of engagement-prone positions, such as *I as a militant who perceives violence as necessary* (see Chapter 3). That is, the majority of I-positions were in strict agreement, reinforcing each other and inclining the militant to the monological side. This is also typical of cognitive closure processes, which occur when individual reasoning and reflection mirror collective justifications and decisions.

Post-revolution militants: popular support

Post-revolution militants believed that many workers supported their actions. For instance, Jaime wondered,

> Has anyone ever asked the workers of the Sacavém Tableware Factory if they agreed that the FP-25 should kill their tyrant? If you had asked them, people would have said "yes", even though they didn't have the courage to do it themselves.

According to the post-revolution militants, they enjoyed this support because they always planned their actions on behalf of, and in solidarity with, the workers. However, Júlia acknowledged that Portugal in the 1980s was a predominantly rural country, so the FP-25's missions truly made sense only to the urban minority in and around Lisbon: "[The campaign] was an expression of the idea of conflict between what we called 'the proletariat' and 'the power-brokers', so it was an eminently urban phenomenon".

Furthermore, the FP-25's popular support ebbed away as its missions became more violent, especially when it started targeting people. As we saw earlier, Júlia initially believed that killing the "symbols of the employers" would encourage the workers to revolt and fight for themselves. However, over time, and particularly after spending some time in prison, her perspective started to change: "The reality proved me wrong; on the contrary, it scared people and made them flee from such situations". Thus, Júlia concluded that her "reading of that social situation" was mistaken, which strengthened the pro-disengagement position *I as a militant who questions the necessity of violence*. We shall explore this further in Chapter 5.

Conclusion

Throughout this chapter, I have demonstrated that an individual's whole life becomes a political issue from the moment when a commitment to a clandestine organisation is made. Personal identity positions are subjugated, giving way to commitment-prone positions fed by affective and cognitive closure processes. The opposite is also true – every political issue becomes the militant's whole life – because the politically motivated events in which they participate construct them as subjects and shape their life stories.

In the three periods of time that are analysed in this study, and sometimes in the specific case of a particular organisation, the dynamics of underground life varied. Pre-revolution militants took underground life most seriously, because the stakes were higher, with a serious risk of both imprisonment and torture. In this sense, they described a very restricted life (e.g., no contact with family or friends) in which they were totally focused on the organisation's objectives. Thus, for these militants, committing one's life to a clandestine organisation was a difficult choice to make which generated conflict among rival I-positions. In order to resolve this conflict and make such a choice, valued personal I-positions (e.g., *I as a student*) had to be subjugated to commitment-prone positions (e.g., *I as someone who believes that armed action is needed to assist the overthrow of the dictatorship*). In some cases, this was achieved through dominance reversal, which entailed no compromise or negotiation among opposing I-positions, but the replacement of counter-commitment positions by pro-commitment positions. This process tended to be supported by centripetal forces, which assembled other I-positions – also known as third positions (e.g., *I as a martyr–hero*) – to mediate the conflict between the counter-commitment and pro-commitment positions.

The challenges of life underground for pre-revolution militants were mitigated by the action of the core position *I as a committed militant*. Through this core position, family-related positions were subjugated and the militant identity was strengthened. Moreover, the bonds of trust among militants were forged by affective closure processes, which contributed to a sense of shared experience and helped to avert interpersonal conflict through the I-position *My comrades as martyr–heroes*. In this context, militants felt that their comrades were sacrificing just as much as, or even more than, themselves.

In pre-revolution organisations, particularly the ARA and the BR, gender was closely related to meso-political narratives. While the ARA followed the PCP's political narrative, which mirrored the country's macro-narrative *Women as housewives*, the BR upheld liberationist, egalitarian and emancipatory principles. This had consequences for the role of women within the various pre-revolution organisations. Some women were expected to play the traditional roles of wife and mother so as not to arouse suspicion (in the ARA), while others participated fully in armed actions (in the BR). However, at times, men's views on women who played a more active role revealed the fine line between women's emancipation through participation in the armed struggle and women's continuing subjugation through serving men's purposes in that struggle.

The experience of living underground for counter-revolution militants differed significantly among the various organisations and in relation to pre- and post-revolution militants. On the one hand, the exiled militants in Spain enjoyed non-clandestine daily life. On the other hand, the militants who remained in Portugal were not overly harassed by the authorities due to the socio-political turmoil that was prevalent in the country at that time. In this context, these militants needed to undergo less identity adaptation than either pre- or post-revolution militants. This may have been related, in part, to the fact that most of the counter-revolution militants were military men who had previously participated in the defence of their country in the Colonial War. Hence, it was likely that identity positions relating to militancy in an armed organisation had already developed. After the revolution, these merely had to be enacted in a slightly different context.

The main challenges faced by counter-revolution militants were related to interpersonal conflict, motivated by power dynamics, and by the difficulty of maintaining tight control over all activities and decisions made by their organisations. Women did not have a place among the counter-revolution militants. At the meso-level, both the ELP and the MDLP echoed the macro-level political narrative *Women as housewives*. Additionally, a number of militants continued to display sexist views regarding women.

In the case of post-revolution militants, life underground was lived differently by different individuals. While some cut all ties with their previous lives from the outset, others maintained a lighter approach motivated by the I-position *I as a human being with emotional needs*. However, when the police investigations intensified, a shielded life underground seemed the best choice to avoid capture. This increased the dominance of the I-position *I as a committed militant*, which became a core position in all of the militants' identity systems. In turn, this core position strengthened other commitment-prone I-positions, such as *I as a loyal comrade*, while subjugating counter-commitment I-positions, such as *I as a mother*. It was also through this core position that challenges were mediated in the underground. Post-revolution militants' narratives focused on stressful daily routines permeated by interpersonal conflict, a lack of resources, and poor logistics. These circumstances often diverted their attention from political goals and led them to concentrate on survival strategies. However, the process of cognitive closure was fed by the militants' detachment from the outside world and by their dependence on the organisation. This strengthened the core position *I as a committed militant*, helped other commitment-prone positions to thrive (e.g., *I as a loyal comrade*), and subjugated disengagement-prone positions (e.g., *My organisation is inefficient and unprepared*).

Both men and women felt that there were sexist attitudes within the FP-25 due to macro-level political narratives which their leftist ideology was unable to override. These could be seen, for instance, in the sexualisation of the role of women within the organisation. Women participated in armed actions, but they were also courted as romantic partners by their male comrades. Post-revolution militants also exploited the cultural position *Portuguese society as utterly sexist* to further their own activities, since women were far less likely to attract police attention than men.

The use of violence also varied across the period under analysis and the different organisations. The pre-revolution militants felt that violence was the only way in which they could express dissent and fight the dictatorship. However, they also adhered to the I-position *I as part of a non-terrorist organisation which does not kill people*. Thus, their violent missions targeted the structures of the regime, not human lives. They believed that this tactic would encourage people to question the established order and support them, rather than fear them and view them as a *terrorist* organisation.

The counter-revolution militants justified their violence as necessary to prevent a perceived threat to the country – specifically, a communist takeover. However, these militants were reluctant to talk about the violent acts their organisations' committed. They preferred to make general statements about their objectives and the actions they could have carried out but chose to veto, because, particularly within the ELP, they held the I-position *I as part of a Catholic organisation which does not commit gratuitous violence*. These militants felt that they enjoyed strong support among the people of northern Portugal and the Catholic Church, which was still seen as a bastion of the deposed regime.

The post-revolution militants were committed to an organisation that openly targeted human lives as a political strategy. They were willing to discuss the thoughts and emotions relating to such violent acts in detail, as well as the voices behind pro-violence I-positions. These included the voice of entitlement, which perceived the organisation's victims as perpetrators; the voice of betrayal, which considered that collaborators with the police had to be punished; and the voice of coercion, which told the militants that they had no other options. Thus, both the centripetal movement of violence-prone positions and cognitive closure processes made post-revolution militants lean to the monological side, keeping their militant identity intact. However, they did not expect their increasingly violent campaign to have a detrimental impact on their popular support, even though a similar pattern has been observed in many other contexts of political violence (see, e.g., Cronin, 2009; Reinares, 2011). The workers felt intimidated and did not want to feel responsible for the bloodshed. In the same way, some of the militants started to question the value of using violence against people, which led to the rise of the pro-disengagement I-positions that are the subject of Chapter 5.

Notes

1 Leila Khaled is a member of the Popular Front for the Liberation of Palestine (PFLP) who achieved worldwide notoriety after participating in two plane hijacks in 1969 and 1970.
2 The Carlist Wars were a series of civil wars that took place in Spain during the nineteenth century. The contenders each intended to establish a separate line of the Bourbon dynasty on the Spanish throne.

References

Carvalho, M. (2017) *Quando Portugal ardeu: histórias e segredos da violência política no pós-25 de Abril*. 3rd Edition. Alfragide: Oficina do Livro.
Cronin, A. K. (2009) *How terrorism ends: understanding the decline and demise of terrorist campaigns*. Princeton, NJ: Princeton University Press.
Dâmaso, E. (1997) *A invasão Spinolista*. Lisbon: Fenda.
della Porta, D. (2013) *Clandestine political violence*. Cambridge: Cambridge University Press.
Hortelão, R., Baêna, L. and Sousa, A. (2012) *Alpoim Calvão: honra e dever*. Porto: Caminhos Romanos.
MacDonald, E. (1991) *Shoot the women first*. London: Arrow Books.
Nacos, B. (2008) 'The portrayal of female terrorists in the media: similar framing patterns in the news coverage of women in politics and in terrorism', in Mahan, S. and Griset, P. (eds) *Terrorism in perspective*. London: Sage Publications, pp. 249–261.
Reinares, F. (2011) 'Exit from terrorism: a qualitative empirical study on disengagement and deradicalization among members of ETA', *Terrorism and Political Violence*, 23(5), pp. 780–803.
Sjoberg, L. and Gentry, C. (2007) *Mothers, monsters, whores: women's violence in global politics*. London: Zed Books.
Torrão, S. (2008) *A mulher portuguesa na guerra e nas forças armadas*. Lisbon: Liga dos Combatentes.

5 Disengagement from a politically violent organisation

> Rewinding to what I experienced in the 1980s, I do not say that if I was twenty years old today I would not do the same thing. Due to my way of seeing society and of being integrated within that society, I am unable to live with injustice, with the arrogance of those who have a uniform or a tie and a pen. I cannot live with it. Now, what will I do? Do you think I'll get away from the police at fifty-seven years old? … I can no longer escape. I am completely aware of this. But that does not stop me from looking at the situations I face every day and saying: "What we need here is the FP-25, or something else, to bring at least some justice regarding what we face every day".
>
> (Jaime from the FP-25)

Disengagement from a politically violent organisation is a very complex process. It involves different motives and options at the individual level and is highly influenced by contextual circumstances. Thus, in this chapter, I present varied and detailed descriptions of the meanings attached to abandoning the militancy of a politically violent organisation. I also focus on the repercussions of such a choice (or imposition), which demands much more than simply stepping away from the organisation (voluntarily or not) and resuming the life that was left at the time of engagement. It demands a restructuring of the individual's identity system from the core position *I as a committed militant* to the I-position *I as a former militant*.

This chapter also serves as a contribution to the highly contested deradicalisation debate. In the past, I have felt inclined to support the distinction between disengagement and deradicalisation on the basis of the assumption that "disengagement focuses on behavioural modification", implying a physical disconnection from the commission of violent activities, while deradicalisation "emphasises an attitudinal change", implying a process of ideology transformation (Reinares, 2011, p. 780). According to this distinction, the essential characteristic of deradicalisation is rejection of the belief that violence is a privileged tool at the service of the political struggle (Ashour, 2009). In this sense, Jaime's comments at the start of this chapter reflect disengagement, but not deradicalisation. However, after studying the life stories of former politically violent militants, I started to see this distinction as less black and white. Many of the former militants I interviewed still held more or less radical views, but they were no longer committed militants. For instance, Jaime still valued his militant identity, but this was counter-balanced by other identity positions (e.g., *I as not agile any more* and *I as a father*). Thus, I now agree with John Horgan (2009, p. 153), who views deradicalisation as "the social and psychological process whereby an individual's commitment to, and involvement in, violent radicalisation is reduced to the extent that they are no longer at risk of involvement and engagement in violent activity".

In this chapter, I explore two aspects of militants' disengagement from a politically violent organisation: ending their commitment to the organisation and the process of reworking the past in the present. I start by looking closely at the reasons they gave for ending their commitment to politically motivated violence, at the incentives for and obstacles against reaching such a decision, and at the pathways they subsequently took. I pay particular attention to how former militants have reintegrated into society. Finally, I explore the ways in which they reflect on their pasts and how they use their memories of past militancy in the present.

Ending commitment to a politically violent organisation

In most cases, across the various periods under analysis and different organisations, the former militants' disengagement was triggered by the dissolution of the organisation. In the cases of pre- and counter-revolution militants, this was usually accompanied by a sense of victory and accomplishment. For the former, the April Revolution brought the *Estado Novo* regime to an end. For the latter, the counter-revolution of 25 November 1975 removed the threat of a communist takeover. Therefore, each organisation wound up its operations because its goals had been achieved. However, some pre- and counter-revolution militants remained committed to their or other causes and kept fighting after the dissolution of their organisations. Others disengaged before the dissolution of their organisations due to a range of organisational and personal factors. The case of the post-revolution militants was different. The FP-25 dissolved because so many of its militants were arrested, killed, or fled abroad. Therefore, a sense of disappointment and frustration is evident in former FP-25 militants' accounts. They are the vanquished. However, some of them insisted that they are not finished yet: they are still working towards socio-political transformation. Thus, in this section, I explore former militants' meaning-making processes regarding their disengagement from politically violent organisations. I take a range of micro-, meso-, and macro-level influences into account, such as changes in personal priorities, how the organisation ended, and socio-political context, respectively.

Furthermore, I examine the former militants' reintegration into mainstream society. I am interested in the shift from pro-commitment to pro-disengagement I-positions and how this influenced the former militants' resumption of their previous lives. I am also interested in how different socio-political contexts of militancy contributed to different levels of reintegration. I argue that specific historical and political circumstances have the capacity either to facilitate or to hinder the reintegration of former politically violent activists.

Pre-revolution militants: disengagement and dissolution of the organisation

The ARA decided to suspend its armed activities in May 1973 because leaders of the PCP considered that the Portuguese political landscape was starting to change. This could be seen, according to Artur, in "new manifestations of struggle", such as progressive Catholics' protests against the Colonial War. In addition, the regime had announced that elections for the National Assembly would be held in October 1973. Subsequently, Artur considered that the ARA was afraid that "the existence of armed action, rather than attracting people, might contribute towards the repressive apparatus and could be used as an excuse for the political police to arrest more people and intensify the repression". Hence, the ARA suspended its operations and never had cause to resume them, given the April Revolution of 1974. The group's former militants were keen to underline that this suspension of activities was simply the result of political analysis of the conditions in the country at the time; it had nothing to do with the arrest of some ARA militants. As Leonel explained:

> It was not like some people thought that we were weakened. No, because there were only six of us in jail, and in total there were about forty of us. Moreover, none of the leaders were in jail. The aim was to suspend in order not to disturb the election campaign. So they could not take advantage of any action to say, "It's all the same" and so on. That could have made the elections difficult.

Leonel then cited an example from the international sphere to justify his organisation's decision, which was supported by the militants: "Near the elections of 1973, the Communist Party suspended the armed struggle to participate in the elections. It was similar to what had happened in Vietnam: the guerrilla war was suspended to participate in the elections and then resumed". Thus, nowadays, former ARA militants seem to feel the need to anchor their identity systems in two positions: one at the meso-level – *The ARA as an armed organisation which did not quit*; and another at the micro-level – *I as former militant who did not quit*. This is particularly relevant in a context in which BR militants – the ARA's rivals who broke with the PCP to create their own armed organisation (see Chapter 1) – claim to be the only ones who maintained a commitment to the armed struggle until the eve of the April Revolution.

In the case of the LUAR, the organisation's dissolution and the disengagement of its militants was a gradual process, as Marco explained: "Nobody conducts an analysis to decree the death of a political organisation. Nobody gets together to say: 'Well, from now on, our store is closed. This is not going anywhere.' Nobody does this. People simply fade away". Other former militants of the LUAR offered a variety of reasons for why they "faded away": the arrest of comrades, including the leader Palma Inácio; some of the organisation's decisions; perceived improvement in the political situation in Portugal, due to Marcelo Caetano's assumption of power; and changes in personal priorities. In this vein, some of the militants' accounts were delivered in a tone of disappointment. For instance, Emílio, who left the organisation before its dissolution, highlighted the fallout from Operation Matias (see Chapter 1 for details). Palma Inácio planned this operation in top secret while in exile. Not even the militants who were tasked with carrying it out knew all the details until they arrived in Portugal. However, they had total confidence in Palma Inácio, who convinced them that it would be a landmark mission, as Emílio recalled:

> [Inácio] appears and doesn't speak about the details of the operation. 'But you'll see that it's an easy thing. We'll have an extraordinary operation. It's not an ordinary operation, small, as we've done so far. It will be something that will be seen around the world.' I thought: 'What can it be? We'll take a small army!' Then, when we were ready to go, we had a number of cars, a few rotten ones … We were all coming down [from France], not knowing what we were going to do, but we thought that there must have been some organised opposition inside the country or something … Then we discovered that everything was glued together with spit … It was another personal disappointment for me.

Instead of seizing control of the city of Covilhã and turning it into a liberated zone, the operation resulted in the arrest of most of the militants who were involved, including Palma Inácio himself. Emílio viewed this as a serious setback for the revolutionary struggle, in general, and the LUAR, in particular. Moreover, he felt that the organisation's leadership was weakened by Palma Inácio's arrest:

> I no longer saw the charisma. Mortágua was fine, but Mortágua is not Palma … Mortágua was a man who was afraid, which is normal, he'd done his share. He was not with us [at Operation Matias]; he was afraid. Hipólito was also afraid. But not Palma – Palma was always there. This man had the charisma to drag us forward.

In these circumstances, Emílio started moving from the I-position *I as someone who fully trusts the organisation's leadership* to *I as someone who no longer sees any charisma in the organisation's leadership*. This centrifugal movement set in motion the disintegration of Emílio's repertoire of identity positions, which had been anchored to the core position *I as a committed militant*.

Furthermore, two other voices influenced the development of Emílio's disengagement-prone positions. The first was the voice of the contextual circumstances within Portugal, which seemed to be changing due to Marcelo Caetano's accession to the premiership in 1968 and his initiation of the Marcelist Spring (see Chapter 1). For Emílio, this seemed to hold "the possibility of modernisation" for Portugal. In his opinion, "a closed institution was disappearing" and "when a society begins to have a certain openness, violence makes fascism worse". The second was the voice of Emílio's career, which strengthened his I-position *I as an academic*. He was not a full-time revolutionary, he had a stable and rewarding job. This served as a stark contrast with the shattered organisation that was the LUAR after the failure of Operation Matias. Thus, Emílio's disengagement was prompted by the decline of his commitment-prone positions, such as *I as someone who fully trusts the organisation's leadership*, and by the increasing centrality of alternative I-positions, such as *I as a militant who is context sensitive* and *I as an academic*. In this vein, just as the process of dominance reversal contributed to the resolution of conflicts between opposing positions promoting engagement with a politically violent organisation (e.g., in the case of Artur presented in Chapter 3), it also contributed to the disengagement of some militants.

Nonetheless, for most of the pre-revolution militants, the April Revolution was the watershed moment that signalled their disengagement from a politically violent organisation. They felt that they had achieved their principal aims: the regime had been overthrown and democracy was being established. Hence, Rui from the ARA considered that the organisation "was no longer necessary, no longer had legitimacy. Even if the ARA's operations were just, they did not have legitimacy in a developing democracy". The majority of BR militants shared this view, as Nuno emphasised: "Fascism had ended. Against whom would we keep planting bombs? It was too violent for us. We needed a very strong cause to be doing that kind of thing. So, it did not make any sense to continue". In addition, Irene considered that after 25 April she could "see people solving their problems and improving their self-esteem, their self-awareness, because they were able to get organised". In this context, she affirmed that the period immediately after the April Revolution was the happiest of her life, because "people were happy". Thus, in August 1974, when BR militants gathered to decide the future of the organisation, most of them voted for disengagement.

The LUAR's militants also saw the April Revolution as the end of armed militancy and a stepping-stone to legal political participation. Henrique, for instance, could not accept political violence in a context of democracy and freedom of expression:

> I have always said – and I made some enemies out there because of this – that everything is justifiable against a dictatorial regime that employs

> force and repression, because there is no alternative. In a regime where there is freedom to say what you think, to organise … I do not accept violence. That's why I've never agreed with those actions that took place after 25 April. It is one thing if I open my mouth and I'm arrested, tortured … but if I can talk without being controlled, if I can convince others of what we need to do, then words are the [best] weapon.

Thus, both the disengagement of most pre-revolution militants and the dissolution of their organisations were triggered by the realisation of their main political aim. In this vein, contextual factors clearly influence not only engagement with but also disengagement from a politically violent organisation. Pre-revolution militants could justify their commitment to an armed organisation only in the context of an authoritarian regime. Such a context, characterised by repression and the exercise of force, as Henrique explained, fed a centripetal movement of engagement-prone positions. It created a logic that there were no other means of expressing dissent and achieving socio-political transformation but through politically violent militancy. By contrast, a context of political freedom encouraged disengagement-prone positions. Militants now felt that other means were available to pursue their socio-political ideals; moreover, these were available to everyone. Thus, in general, pre-revolution militants were able to disengage from politically motivated violence and maintain the continuity of their identity systems through the I-position *I as a militant who achieved his/her aims.*

Pre-revolution militants: reintegration into society

Pre-revolution militants reported few difficulties in relation to their reintegration into society. This seems largely due to the fact that the politically motivated violence that occurred during the *Estado Novo* regime was not criminally prosecuted after the April Revolution. Thereby, the militants were free to return to their previous lives. Artur from the ARA, for instance, confirmed that he had "an excellent transition". He started by reconnecting with family and friends immediately after the revolution and then easily resumed life above ground. He recognised, though, that other people found it more difficult to abandon their clandestine identities: "they kept using pseudonyms as if they were still underground". However, these were temporary difficulties relating to adapting personal identity systems to a new reality. Overall, the militants were ecstatic. Xavier, from the ARA, affirmed that the April Revolution was the most important event of his life because it allowed him to return from exile and reconnect with his family:

> They knew who I was, and while this regime lasted I could never return to Portugal, nor have a normal life in Portugal … My mother suffered a bit with that. She used to say: "While this lasts, I cannot see my son. I will die and I will not see my son!" And it wasn't one; there

> were two sons. I was fleeing from the police and my brother was fleeing from the Colonial War. So, 25 April brought such joy to my mother and to me.

A few militants joined different political organisations after the April Revolution. Some of these were legal, such as the PRP/BR, while others were clandestine, like the FP-25. Diogo from the LUAR joined the PRP/BR because he agreed with its principles and liked the fact that it "was run by a woman". For him, this was "totally new". However, he left the organisation after just three years, because he did not agree with its strategy of funding itself through bank robberies:

> After 1977, the PRP/BR became an organisation that conducted robberies, and I was not okay with that, with the robberies. They were aimed at paying employees! I was never paid by any party, nor any union. I was never any organisation's employee.

Moreover, another militant, Humberto, who was a member of the PRP/BR before joining the FP-25, revealed that this strategy proved problematic for the former organisation for another reason. He knew of several militants who had fought with the BR before the April Revolution and had not subsequently disengaged. The organisation was unsure about the consequences of the April Revolution, so it preferred to keep a few militants on standby during the first years of democracy. They remained underground in Portugal or went into hiding abroad and survived by robbing banks. However, most of them were eventually arrested, including several PRP/BR leaders, who tried to conceal their illegal activities from the authorities. According to Humberto, the leaders then instructed the surviving clandestine militants to "keep quiet because they were trying to negotiate an amnesty". This directive was not well received by the militants who remained at large, including Humberto. He recalled thinking:

> Fuck them! Until then, we were ordered to do things. Now we were ordered to keep quiet? … People had been radicalised and now they could not radicalise any more … So, people said: "Let's break with this and join a different story [the FP-25]".

Thus, the clandestine militants faced a stark choice: either continue to fight or go to prison and pay for the crimes they had committed since the April Revolution. As Humberto explained,

> They did not want to get caught, so they needed to find different organisational solutions, because the PRP was no longer responsive, because the leaders of the PRP were all in jail, or at least the majority of them. The FP-25 was born there.

The BR interviewees had a slightly different view of this situation. Lídia, a co-founder of the BR and one of the leaders of the PRP/BR, felt that the militants who left the PRP/BR and joined the FP-25 simply did not know what else to do. They had engaged with the armed struggle from a very young age, and the April Revolution had left a significant void in their lives. One way of filling this void was to engage with another organisation. Thus, Lídia believed there was a micro-level explanation for the defection of some PRP/BR militants to the FP-25 (the personal choices of those militants), rather than a meso-level explanation (the path chosen by the PRP/BR after the April Revolution). Such a view might be justified by the persistence of valued I-positions among some BR militants, particularly its founders, regarding the use of violence. Some pre-revolution militants continued to pride themselves on adhering to the I-position *I as part of a non-terrorist organisation which does not kill people.* This position helped them to live comfortably with their past militancy. From their perspective, they were not members of a terrorist organisation, because they did not kill people. Moreover, they fought for freedom in the context of a dictatorial regime. In this scenario, recognising that the PRP/BR's activities after the April Revolution left some militants with few options and prompted them to engage with another organisation that *did* kill people within a democracy would challenge their position *We as good militants who do not kill people* (the BR), which counterposed the position *They as bad militants who do kill people* (the FP-25).

Counter-revolution militants: disengagement and dissolution of the organisation

Most of the counter-revolution militants also disengaged as a result of the dissolution of their respective organisations. These dissolutions were triggered by the 25 November 1975 counter-revolution, which ended the Ongoing Revolutionary Process and launched the Ongoing Constitutional Process (see Chapter 1). In the case of the MDLP, for instance, General Spínola announced the dissolution of the organisation after the events of 25 November. This generated two distinct reactions among the militants: some rejoiced and started making plans to return to Portugal and resume their previous lives; others did not agree with the directive and vowed to continue the struggle on their own.

Sérgio and Daniel were in the first group. Sérgio received Spínola's announcement with great joy: "I agreed immediately. I accepted immediately. For me, it was a relief … in the sense that … I really wanted to go back to Portugal. I was so homesick, I really wanted to return to Portugal". Daniel also accepted the announcement without question. For these militants, the events of 25 November meant that they were suddenly free to return to Portugal and resume their lives, as Daniel explained: "After 25 November, the MDLP was simply extinguished. It was over and would never be heard of again. In fact, everyone – or almost everyone – who was in the MDLP in Spain after 25 November ended up moving back". He continued:

> When there was freedom after 25 November – a new freedom, like the one after 25 April – the people concerned – or most of them – withdrew from politics. All the Spínolist military were never heard of again. I withdrew completely from politics … [and] most of the people who were with me in Spain never engaged in politics again.

As with the pre-revolution militants, this sudden disengagement from politically motivated activities, both violent and non-violent, seemed to be motivated by the fact that the militants felt that they had achieved their principal aim, as Ilídio explained: "After 25 November we shut the door and left … Communism had not entered Portugal". Thus, they could get on with their lives, underlined by the valued I-position *I as a militant who achieved his/her aims*, which gave their identity systems a degree of continuity.

However, as already mentioned, a few MDLP militants did not disengage at the time of the dissolution of the organisation. Some disengaged militants, including Dinis, suggested that such decisions were motivated by financial hardship: "A number of MDLP operatives were unemployed and still had weapons, so they decided to act on their own". In the same vein, Sérgio recalled that the organisation had paid these militants, but their salaries had ceased upon its dissolution, which caused "many MDLP elements to become genuine outlaws who conducted robberies and so on, [supposedly] on behalf of the MDLP, which no longer existed". He concluded that such behaviour cast "a dark shadow after the fall of the MDLP". From being categorised as militants, the individuals who did not disengage started to be viewed as "bandits who may have participated in the MDLP but who were now out of control".

Unsurprisingly, those militants who remained active after the dissolution of the organisation told a rather different story. Álvaro revealed that he was a member of a group of half a dozen militants who decided to carry on because they believed there was still "a score to settle" with "those who made the revolution", particularly the PCP. These militants were convinced that they were targeted by the new regime purely because their political views leaned towards those of the *Estado Novo*, as Álvaro explained:

> They never had proof that I placed whatever it was [explosives], but I was held in prison for four months without charge. Let me say this, in Salazar's time, you could be held for only ninety days plus ninety. Today, you can be held for three years without trial. What democracy is this?

Thus, Álvaro's political narrative centred on his grievances with the April Revolution and the new regime. Those grievances were fed not only by past events but also by the economic hardship that Portugal was suffering at the time of our conversation (early 2013). In his opinion, that hardship could be traced all the way back to the April Revolution and the political landscape it created. During our conversation, he repeatedly compared the democratic present with the *Estado Novo*, seeing the latter as the much better option. Therefore, from Álvaro's point of view, disengaging from the struggle would have meant abandoning his dream of a counter-revolution that would reinstate the *Estado Novo*. He did eventually stop committing violent actions, although this decision was not motivated by any softening of his political views. Indeed, if anything, these became more radical over time. However, he found it increasingly difficult to subjugate the voice of responsibility towards his family, which called upon the I-position *I as a father*:

> Today, we no longer think about it [armed struggle]. I have two children and the reasoning is that if I am here talking to you today, it's because I have children, because I am responsible. They did not ask to be born and I have no right to make them follow me and visit me in prison, leaving them marginalised, without a father. However, it is only for this reason, because I have no respect … I respect some people, not many. No one is to blame for being poor, but all are guilty of being stupid.

Counter-revolution militants: reintegration into society

In terms of reintegration into society after the dissolution of the MDLP, different militants had different experiences, according to their type of involvement with the organisation. Those in Spain, in general, opted to wait a few months before returning to Portugal to ensure that they would not face criminal charges. Sérgio's wife returned ahead of him and contacted the military to ask if his return would mean his arrest. It was agreed that he would face desertion charges, but he would not be arrested. Other militants opted to extend their exile in other countries, since Spain was notified to extradite all members of the MDLP. For instance, Ilídio delayed his return to Portugal for two years after the dissolution of the organisation. The situation was simpler for the MDLP militants who were based in Portugal because they had never been identified by the authorities, so they had no charges to answer. For instance, Dinis had maintained his military career throughout his membership of the MDLP and never suffered any consequences. Finally, some of the militants who chose to continue after the dissolution of the MDLP were brought to justice and a number of them served prison sentences.

Afonso's case typifies most of the counter-revolution militants' experiences concerning their reintegration into society:

> In January 1976 I returned to Portugal. A member of the Revolutionary Council said I could return. I went to Lisbon and after some time I went

> to Caxias, where my file was closed without any reprisals. I was cleared of all illegal activity.

This response from the authorities generated grievances that have persisted in Portuguese society until the present day, because there is a sense that the counter-revolution militants received preferential treatment, especially in comparison with the FP-25. For instance, the vast majority of them did not have to appear in court and answer for a campaign that had involved violence against property and people. This led Bruno, an FP-25 militant, to suggest that, while the justice system did not treat the FP-25 unfairly, "it treated the right better".

Post-revolution militants: disengagement and dissolution of the organisation

When I asked Júlia how she disengaged from the organisation, she bluntly answered: "There are two types of FP-25 militants: those who were arrested and those who fled abroad". She was in the first category. Her simple answer is an accurate reflection of what became of all of the post-revolution militants – the final consequence of their commitment to a politically violent organisation. However, as the interview process continued, I started to appreciate the full scope of disengagement in the life of a militant and realised that it entailed far more than either arrest or exile. These were merely the final outcomes of a long and complex process.

For most militants, the substantial amount of time they spent away from mainstream society and the hardships of life underground made them start amending their priorities and, subsequently, their I-positions. Mariana, for instance, eventually grew tired of running and wanted to stop. This was reinforced by the fact that she became pregnant and decided to keep the baby, prioritising the I-position *I as a mother*. It seems likely that this decision was at least partly motivated by her exhaustion, because she had been pregnant before but had decided to have an abortion.

Similarly, despite knowing that she could not simply "go back", as time went by Júlia started to give more weight to previously subjugated I-positions that brought her closer to an imagined return to life above ground. She stopped participating directly in violent missions, which supported the emergence of the new I-position *I as a non-active member of the FP-25*: "I said I couldn't continue to participate in actions … and in practice I hardly got involved anymore". Most of the voices that fed this position were associated with a weakening in her identification with the organisation, which brought the important internal position *I as someone who does not identify with the role of a militant* to the fore:

> The truth is that I never felt like a guerrilla militant, in the sense that I always had the perception that my skills in terms of training, knowledge, and know-how were infinitely below what would be reasonable and necessary for the kind of proposal we put forward.

Júlia's waning commitment to the organisation also called upon the external position *My organisation is inefficient and unprepared*:

> We started lame and we never recovered in two ways: in the sense of reflection on what we were doing and what we wanted to do; and in the sense of the means we employed to carry out the actions.

Thus, the emergence of Júlia's centrifugal positioning was closely associated with a fracturing of her personal identification with the organisation's goals and its capacity to effect socio-political transformation. Beyond the failure of the militants' training, she linked the organisation's inefficiency to an absence of collective reflection regarding goals, planning, and action. This led to ever more self-focused guilt regarding unsuccessful actions, particularly those that claimed the lives of comrades, which at the same time fed the centrifugal I-positions that encouraged Júlia's disengagement. For her, the death of comrades in confrontations with the police were "a tsunami within the organisation", "an earthquake" that caused "an extremely strong sense of guilt", because she considered that "a good proportion of the deaths occurred due to clear operational failure".

This seems to have supported Júlia's gradual distancing from the FP-25 and motivated a process of dominance reversal within her I-positions. The previously dominant I-position *I as a committed militant* was relegated to the background as she started to prioritise the interests of her family. This gave voice to the *I as a mother* and *I as a partner* I-positions, which in turn led to the adoption of new behaviours that compromised her clandestine life:

> My partner was arrested while robbing a bank … He was injured – shot – and went to hospital … I was living underground. They were all arrested in that action and I said: "I'm going to visit the block. I don't care."

Nevertheless, as mentioned at the beginning of this section, Júlia fully disengaged from the FP-25 only when she was arrested. This was because the I-position *I as a loyal comrade* fed her commitment to the organisation (see Chapter 4), reinforced her belief that she "needed to honour the memory of the comrades who had died", and keep fighting for her imprisoned comrades. Thus, she stayed aboard, waiting for the ship to sink, as she knew it would:

> Stupidly, we stayed. And it was really stupid because there was nothing to do. We just waited to be arrested. [But] I would not say that I regret it. I don't know if my path would necessarily have been different if I'd gone abroad … I don't know if it would have been better. So, we stayed and we put up with prison.

Humberto was also emotionally affected by the deaths of comrades. In addition, he started fearing for his own life. This voice of fear gave rise to the I-position *I as a militant who is afraid of being killed*, which prompted his disengagement from the organisation. He felt that they were robbing ever more banks just to keep the organisation going. However, in his opinion, it was not worth risking his life to rob a bank, and this conviction grew when some of his comrades lost their lives during robberies:

> These things started hitting hard with the start of the repression, the arrests, the deaths … I mean we seemed to leave everything behind just to get money. Rob some shitty corner banks? These were things that made no sense to anyone … People were not there to rob small banks. They wanted to do other things … things that were significant to them.

Post-revolution militants: amnesty

Long-standing differences within the organisation, the absence of a viable alternative, and the high number of arrests led the majority of imprisoned FP-25 militants to support the amnesty proposal (see Chapter 1). Humberto believed that this "was not opportunistic or motivated by the pressure of those who were in jail and wanted to get out". In fact, he considered that the majority of militants "learned from the experience and paid the price".

Several other militants similarly suggested that the threat of arrest came to be viewed as a price to be paid for their militancy. This was manifested in the I-position *I as a militant who has to pay the price for my militancy.* According to Júlia, "[t]he price of requesting the amnesty … is an apology. Look at it in whatever way you wish, but it's the person recognising their wrongdoing, and that has a price in people's heads". Thus, in order to look herself in the mirror and feel comfortable in her own skin for the rest of her life, she could not accept the amnesty. She had to see her militancy through to the end. She had to pay the price by completing her prison sentence. Besides, she did not believe that the militants' identities – who they were and what they believed in – had to dissolve through their acceptance of an amnesty merely because their organisation was dissolving:

> Is it true that the organisation had no future? It is! The organisation was shattered, that's true. But it's one thing for the organisation to be shattered and something else for people to assume that their attitudes were wrong … To all intents and purposes, accepting an amnesty meant the former was a fact.

Thereby, Júlia still showed clear traces of the I-position *I as a committed militant*. Such a key identity position rarely disappears completely overnight. Rather, it slowly gives ground to both previously subjugated and new positions, making its way, gradually, to the periphery. Thus, when confronted with the possibility of accepting an amnesty and resuming her role as a mother – as her parents (who were looking after her three children) encouraged her to do – Júlia once again prioritised her political convictions and completed her full prison sentence. Jaime, Júlia's partner and the father of her two younger children, made the same choice. He also believed that he had to pay his debt to society in full, so no one could accuse him of anything after he left jail. In addition, he felt that this was the only way of facilitating a smooth integration into mainstream society, and particularly into politics.. Although Jaime did not present this as an easy decision to make, he viewed it as essential to maintain his sense of identity:

> You suddenly see the doors opening, everyone leaving, but you stay, because you would not sign a piece of paper. You have your dignity. I owe nothing to society. Therefore, I consider myself an activist, a political activist, who was with others in the political struggle until the end of the fight. I risked it all and, suddenly, I lost. I lost and that defeat equated to ten years in prison. But I left without owing anything to society because I served my sentence until the end. I did not get out with a pardon or an amnesty. I left after serving my time. I served it all. I owe nothing to society.

Post-revolution militants: reintegration into society

A number of post-revolution militants described the challenges of resuming "normal life" after serving a long prison sentence. Some of these accounts suggested that incarceration came close to ruining their lives. Júlia, for instance, focused on the practical aspects of returning to mainstream society, such as having a criminal record but no money, no job, and no home. Moreover, in some cases, including Júlia's, children were involved. She described "starting adult life with a ten-year delay".

Bruno also mentioned the material "damage" that is suffered by the full-time revolutionary:

> Who suffered the damage? It was our loss. At the age twenty I was chief of a journalists' bureau and had two cars. Then I became a revolutionary and lost these things. Now, I own a house for the first time after all these years, you know? I have fifteen years of social security contributions, all made in the last years of my life.

Furthermore, this interviewee felt that his militancy had a negative impact on his emotional well-being:

> I've been married three times already. I have children with four different women. I've reorganised my life about five or six times. This was not what I planned, right? I would have stayed with the first woman, probably would have had three or four children, and would have been a guy with a perfectly normal life.

In this vein, both Júlia and Bruno felt that their decision to become a politically violent militant had a profoundly disruptive effect on their life course. For them, life was not all it could have been.

This sense of disruption, which was found primarily among the post-revolution militants, seemed to be linked to the collective position *We as part of an organisation which was defeated*. This position gave voice to the militants' disappointment and frustration over the organisation's lack of success and their own imprisonment. A mournful Bruno insisted that the FP-25 "did not change anything" because "we lost" and "the workers did not assimilate" the reasons for the organisation's struggle. According to Júlia, this frustration led many former FP-25 militants to abandon politics completely and simply try to get on with their lives:

> I think that all militants who were in prison left deeply frustrated and, in most cases, unable to restart. I don't know about everyone, but as far as I know, most people did not get involved socially and, therefore, decided to deal with life in a commonplace, everyday manner.

However, this was not the case with Júlia's partner, Jaime. As a result of his past militancy, and because he devoted his "period of greater physical strength" to the political struggle and suffered the consequences with dignity (by paying his debt to society rather than accepting an amnesty), he developed the I-position *I as a former militant who is still civically and politically active*: "I have this need to feel that I am contributing with whatever I do, be it at local political meetings, at the Left Bloc [political party] or at work". Thus, Jaime's narrative identity was marked by continuity I-positions. The same could be said of his views regarding the use of violence to solve social problems, which he articulated in the following hypothetical story:

> Sometimes I ask myself what I would do if I were working for a company in which some agent of capital, be it an administrator or an employer, created a famine … I would have two paths: I could endure the situation … but there would be another path that I, personally, would never follow. I would never kill myself. [If I were to die], he [the administrator or the employer] would go first, then I would go. He goes before me. He has to go before me. I cannot leave him there … the person who has created my situation … If I had no money to eat or to pay the rent, would I put a rope around my own neck? No, before putting a rope around my neck, I would have to put it around the neck of someone else. That is evident.

Jaime told this story in the context of the economic crisis that Portugal was suffering at the time of our interview, at the start of 2013. And he was not the only interviewee to display the I-position *I as a former militant who still thinks that violence is defensible.* Mariana also argued that violence was justified in some sectors of contemporary Portuguese society. However, like Jaime in the quote that opened this chapter, she had no plans to perpetrate it herself:

> I have no regrets. I did what had to be done and I'm not sorry at all … I am the same person, by the way. I'm still here. I'm not sorry. I got tired – that's different. I'm not sorry, my ideas are the same, my fight is the same … I still think violence is defensible. But we got old. If I was still twenty years old, they would see!

In this vein, it is important to note that disengagement from a politically violent organisation does not always imply a full transformation of the former militant's identity system. Of course, such a transformation can take place, as we shall see in the next section, but some disengaged individuals, including Jaime and Mariana, retain the identity positions that led to their engagement in a politically violent organisation in the first place. However, other factors, such as age or a shift in personal priorities, usually inhibit recidivism, as Jaime acknowledged when I asked whether he still believes that political violence is the best way to solve socio-political problems:

> People often say: "We need the FP-25 again", I answer: "Comrade, whoever wants the fruit should climb the tree. I have already climbed the tree … I fell and broke a leg, so I am no longer available for that. I no longer have the physical strength for that type of activity. I have a granddaughter. [But] whoever wants it should go for it!"

The past reworked in the present

In this section, I explore how former politically violent militants frame and recount their reflections on the past. I shall demonstrate that their current identity positions are entangled with perceptions of their past militancy, and explain how the past may or may not provide unity and purpose in the present. As we saw earlier, former militants' identity systems are not static; rather, they evolve in accordance with the various spatial, temporal, and relational dimensions that individuals inhabit throughout their lives. Therefore, throughout this section, we find both continued and discontinued identity positions in the accounts of former militants: some are very proud of their past activities and believe that they have not changed too much; others are more ambivalent about the choices they have made and wonder if they should have chosen a different path; and a third group feel that they have left their militancy behind and are significantly different from the people they used to be.

Pre-revolution militants: reflections on the past

A few pre-revolution militants hinted that their perception of the past was the whole point of my research. For instance, Irene from the BR was keen to emphasise the I-position *I as a proud former militant*: "I'm quite proud to think that I did something like that. It's a choice that pleases me very much". She also presented herself as someone who had maintained her core values over time, despite some evolution:

> What I did in the past was me. I mean, it was me with my beliefs, my values and my way of being in the world. And now it is the same. I mean, I strive, I fight … to be strong, to be true to my beliefs, my values … which have not changed much. They have become more specific, more elaborated.

This position of *I as someone who kept my core values* was also articulated by Marco from the LUAR, who affirmed: "I can never get away from the past". He believed that he could not become someone he has never been, although, like Irene, he felt his current thinking was "a little more worked". Nevertheless, his core values had never altered: "My hatred regarding those who exploit others remains the same. This includes those who are now exploiting others and who in the past said they were against the exploiters". Thereby, for Marco, "it would be hypocritical to say: 'I think differently today'. It would be hypocrisy because no one can make a break with the past". In this vein, a number of pre-revolution militants displayed a strong sense of retaining the same essential views over time – the same identity, the same disapproval of social injustice, and the same willingness to defend their ideals in a democratic context, through democratic means. In this context, Henrique from the LUAR also affirmed his pride regarding his current life, because he had remained faithful to his principles, which were reflected in his ongoing activism: "I have great pride in my present – the same as or more than in my past … I still do the same as I used to do – not in the same way, but I continue to fight for my goals".

Although pre-revolution militants expressed pride in their pasts and believed that they had retained their core values, they simultaneously acknowledged that there had been some revision of their socio-political views. This acknowledgement seemed to be key to maintaining a sense of continuity between their past and present positions. Despite believing that their core values and views had remained largely consistent and that there were still palpable injustices in Portuguese society, these militants were no longer willing to engage in the armed struggle. This can be explained through the meta-position *I as a reflective former militant*. Through this meta-position, the former militants had come to terms with their continued disengagement from the armed struggle. It had left them with the impression that they had attained "more worked", "more specific", "more elaborated" versions of themselves. This meta-position was clearly at work in Lídia's life, giving voice to her reinterpretation of history. Her reflection on the previous forty years had made her question "the possibility of establishing a revolutionary socialist project" – a project she had supported in the past. Looking back at her militancy in the BR and the PRP/BR, she admitted that her ideas had been "too simplistic". However, she recognised that it was easy to make this evaluation with the benefit of hindsight and her personal experience of being a militant herself: "We had little regard for the circumstances of the defeat of the Russian Revolution and the causes of that defeat. We had little regard for the evolution towards Stalinism and for the economic circumstances in the world". Thus, Lídia – and a number of other former militants – acknowledged that one can become blind to some aspects of reality when living and acting in a certain historical moment. Yet, in the years following their militancy, these former militants were able to reflect on the various factors that had been at play in the past, because they could see it from the perspective of the present. They gained access not only to their own stories but also to "larger stories" (Randall, 2010, p. 151). For Lídia, it was key to situate her own militancy, and particularly her decision to disengage from political violence, in the broader historical context. Although the April Revolution attained one of the goals she had fought for – the end of the *Estado Novo* regime – it did not lead to socialism. Nevertheless, Lídia adopted and maintained pro-disengagement positions, because her political reasoning was assessed in relation to other historical events and experiences around the world.

Pre-revolution militants: us versus them

The core identity position *I as part of a non-terrorist organisation which does not kill people*, which was evident in the period of activity within a politically violent organisation, was retained after disengagement from the armed struggle. Yet, its function within the self changed slightly. In their period of activity, pre-revolution militants would use this position to seek popular support, as described in Chapter 4. Later, they would use it to highlight the clear distinction between the non-terrorist actions committed by their pre-revolution organisations and the terrorist actions of other organisations. All of the pre-revolution militants were keen to stress that they vehemently refused terrorism. For them, this meant no targeting of human life, even among their perceived enemies. However, the regime insisted on labelling them "terrorists", which, according to Nuno from the BR, was a deliberate strategy aimed at "scaring off possible support that could be given to the struggle". From Nuno's perspective, "terrorism is one thing; fighting against an unjust government is quite another". Xavier from the ARA articulated a similar distinction when he asked with a sneering grin: "Have you already talked with people from other *terrorist* groups?" He preferred to call ARA militants "vigilantes". In his opinion, the label "terrorism" tends to be used both to benefit those in power and to discredit those who fight for political change:

> Israelis are now more terroristic than the Palestinians, but as the latter wanted independence, they used to be accused of terrorism by the English and others who wanted to take control of the territory … So, what is terrorism depends on your point of view.

However, Xavier's attitude changed when he turned his attention to militants who kill people and are labelled "terrorists" as a result. For him, such terrorism "is in the blood" and totally different from his militancy in the ARA:

> We were not crazy or fanatical like the guys walking around in the Middle East. No! Those guys intend to die; they are not afraid of death. They have explosives around their waists. It is fanaticism. They aim to go to heaven, but we knew we were not going to heaven! If we died, we knew we were going into the ground. We used to joke: "We have no right to heaven!"

Xavier's assessment of Middle Eastern jihadists echoed mainstream descriptions of these politically violent militants, who are routinely depicted as "kooks, crazies, demented, or at best misguided" (Zulaika and Douglass, 1996, p. 62). Therefore, he drew a clear line between *us* – armed militants who did not intend to kill others or themselves – and *them* – armed militants who are motivated by "fanaticism" to kill both others and themselves. Moreover, his use of the word "fanaticism" resonated with the common perception that Middle Eastern violent militants are motivated purely by religion. Such a motivation clashed with his own I-position *I as an atheist.* Xavier could not imagine committing violent acts to earn a place in heaven, because he did not believe in heaven. Thus, in the absence of a plausible perceived motivation, he chose to follow the storylines that he read and heard in the mainstream media, which highlighted the "fanaticism" of contemporary militants.

Pre-revolution militants also commented on the violent actions committed by counter- and post-revolution organisations in Portugal, which they viewed as absolutely illegitimate. The ELP and the MDLP were criticised for employing violence, including assassinations, when democracy was taking its first steps. Moreover, Rui from the ARA suggested that the Catholic Church supported such violence: "A bomb in downtown Coimbra, the death of the priest and the Catholic Church behind the operations with Canon Melo's hands full of blood".

In regard to the FP-25, Rui felt that the problem was not the targets, who "were truly fascists", but the strategy: murder. In Rui's opinion, this strategy invariably damages the image of the political struggle and the left-wing, even if the targets are legitimate:

> The FP-25 killed a man in Sacavém. That man was a scoundrel, he deserved to die five hundred times, but that operation never should have happened because … in the collective consciousness it called into

> question the nature of a left which wanted to be necessary, which wanted to be fair and ethical.

Rui supported this opinion by citing Lenin, particularly his book *The Childhood Disease of Communism*. This book covers "the nonsense committed with the best of intentions, and that sometimes is tragic". Rui felt that the FP-25's militants, as Marxist–Leninists, should have consulted it, but "unfortunately many people have not read it". On the same topic, Irene from the BR added that killing factory owners "cannot be justified in any way because there was already freedom. People could talk and if someone had to put the man out of there, dead or alive, it was the factory workers, not the FP-25". As a result, the pre-revolution militants viewed the FP-25's adherence to violent strategies in a democratic environment as inappropriate.

Counter-revolution militants: reflections on the past

The counter-revolution militants' accounts also revealed that they felt they made the right choices in the 1970s. For instance, Ilídio from the MDLP declared that "all actions made sense". For him, stopping communism was a cause "worth fighting for". Moreover, although he admitted that he had made some changes over the years, he felt that the essential characteristics of his identity remained the same: "You know, some things that I did … I think I did very well … [but that] does not mean that I did not have to adapt … But, basically, I have not changed one centimetre". When I asked him to elaborate, he replied: "I don't change because these things are cemented within me and I see no reason to change". His use of the word "cemented" is very interesting. It implies consolidation, reinforcement over time. It represents Ilídio's perception of the crystallisation process of his self, which was modelled on his father's, grandfather's, and great-grandfather's selves. They all shared the same name, as well as the same rigorous principles, which Ilídio illustrated with a number of stories:

> My grandfather refused to follow the Republic and was arrested for refusing to take the oath. My great-grandfather on my mother's side was also a military man. Once he went with his son to collect some shoes from the shoemaker and the kid stole some nails. The shoemaker saw him do it but said nothing. When they got home, my great-grandfather asked: "What have you got in your hand? Where did you get those nails from?" He forced him to go back and apologise … My father used to tell a story about his return from Brazil with a certain sadness. He had been away for twelve years and when he arrived home my grandfather was on the porch reading a newspaper. My father said: "Good morning, sir." My grandfather did not stop reading his newspaper. He just said: "Good morning. Pleasant journey?" My father felt sad about this episode, but it was a lesson about values, you know? Values that remained firm within me.

Like Afonso (see Chapter 4), Ilídio displayed the I-position *I as someone who had an austere upbringing*. This and the values it inculcated influenced these militants' life stories, serving as the foundations on which their identity systems were built over time. Ilídio was able to recall and relate these stories in his late seventies, demonstrating their resilience throughout his life.

Other counter-revolution militants evaluated the past with less certainty. Sérgio, for instance, displayed the I-position *I as a former militant who doubts the merit of my past choices*. In his opinion, his militancy had negative consequences at both the professional and the personal level. Professionally, he fought in the courts for years to secure official recognition for his military career. Personally, he preferred not to discuss the consequences, but he clearly suffered a difficult reintegration into society, including some mental health issues. His doubts increased when he compared his choice of militancy to those of his peers, who had simply continued with their ordinary lives. He viewed the past from the perspective of the present, just as Lídia from the BR did:

> There is a question, which is: knowing what I know today, with the knowledge I have today, would I have continued to make war and so on … would I have continued to be a militant, to spend those years of my life … which caused my current problems? … Others have much bigger problems, the stress of war and so on … It is very difficult to answer, right?

However, in contrast to Lídia, Sérgio was unable to develop a meta-position to integrate his past, present, and imagined future, which would have allowed him to create new meanings to maintain the coherence of his self. As a result, he lived with the uncertainty of what might have been if he had made different life choices, such as rejecting politically violent militancy: "Today, I sometimes think that it would have been better to leave and remain quiet, like others who maintained their positions and did not get into trouble".

Daniel also reflected on how his life might have been if he had chosen not to join the MDLP. However, he reached the conclusion that his choice and the experiences of his youth made him happy. During our interview, it was clear that he still leaned on the I-position *I as a young idealist*, which had previously helped him maintain his commitment to a politically violent organisation (see Chapter 4). This position allowed him to look back and integrate his past militancy within his present self as a normative experience. In coalition with this position, strengthening the coherence of his narrative identity, he displayed the I-positions *I as a proud former militant* and *I as someone who accomplished the goals of my youth*. Thereby, he felt that he protected his country from a dreadful fate. In so doing, he sacrificed some areas of his life. However, he attained his goals and insisted he would do it all again:

> If a person is not an idealist at twenty-five, if we do not fight for what we believe in, do not sacrifice our life … I was one of the best students at the Law Faculty in Coimbra. A professor gave me letters of recommendation for the best law firms in Brazil. If I had gone to Brazil at that time, I would have had a fantastic life and today I would be Brazilian. But I decided to stay and live almost as a beggar … Do you know what it's like to live with a wife and two children in a single room? I did that for idealism, for pure idealism, nothing else. So, I think one should have idealism when one is very young. If I went back … I would do exactly the same thing, even knowing what I know today, because this is one of the things that makes me proud in my life: fighting for what I believed in, fighting against something that I thought was very dangerous for my country.

Sérgio and Daniel had both contemplated a range of possible selves over the years. However, Sérgio had been unable to solve the conflict between his real and imagined positions, while Daniel, despite recognising that his life could have been very different, had managed to justify his past militancy and integrate it in his evolving life story. The latter might have been aided by the fact that he had never been in the military and his disengagement from the organisation, return to Portugal, and resumption of his previous life had been a relatively straightforward process. As his militancy had little effect on the rest of his life, he was able to deal with it quite comfortably. By contrast, Sérgio could not escape the conclusion that his past militancy caused him much more harm than good. After almost four decades, he was still at odds with his own narrative identity, constantly questioning his past choices.

Counter-revolution militants: the MDLP versus the ELP

Only MDLP militants had something to say about the ELP. They felt that the latter organisation occupied a much more prominent position in the Portuguese imaginary of the political violence carried out by right-wing groups, as Sérgio explained:

> Even today, you can still see remnants of the ELP on walls [i.e., graffiti] … The ELP had a major impact on Portuguese public opinion when they were in Spain and making a near-zero contribution in terms of execution, right? The psychological part was ELP, ELP, ELP.

Sérgio offered two possible explanations for this situation. First, the ELP's acronym. When said in Portuguese, "ELP" sounds like the English word "help", contributing to the image of an organisation that would save the nation from communism: "Only the name is amazing, isn't it?" Second, the ELP's propaganda campaign, which emulated those of more established politically violent organisations: "They held a press conference hooded like

ETA, which had a huge impact and made the front pages of the newspapers". Thus, according to Sérgio, the ELP became a major player in the imagination of the Portuguese public, who cast it as a "bogeyman", declaring, "Look out, the ELP is coming!" However, he stressed that the ELP was a much smaller and less "credible" organisation than the MDLP. Hence, he felt it was deplorable that the ELP sometimes claimed responsibility for violent actions that were actually the work of the MDLP. Ilídio added that the ELP hoped to achieve the impossible: "A return to the past … to a regime like the *Estado Novo*".

Post-revolution militants: reflections on the past

Júlia and Jaime, whom I interviewed separately, raised interesting points in relation to their reflections on the past. Jaime displayed a clear coalition of positions that reified his past militancy, including the I-position *I as a proud former militant*:

> I always remember the past from the perspective of saying: "For better or worse, I stepped forward and reached the highest level of the political struggle". When the political activist uses violence, I think it is the final phase of the political struggle. I lost, but the causes that led me – the feeling that led me – to this final phase of the political struggle was exactly the feeling of being in an unjust society, a society in which those who are unable to defend themselves always end up victimised.

This position was reinforced by *I as a former militant who cherishes his past memories*:

> Unlike Júlia, who basically does not like to talk about the past or remember the things that are behind her, I like it. I like to remember the route [I took] because it is a path that gives me some knowledge to change things.

Finally, Jaime also displayed the I-position *I as someone who retained my core values*: "You are face to face with someone who, despite everything, with respect to his social, ideological and civic participation, maintains the same posture he had twenty-five years ago".

By contrast, Júlia had little interest in reflecting on the past. She confirmed that Jaime talks a lot about their past militancy and "remembers every action, every situation, specific situations". However, Júlia herself "somehow blacked out a little". Unlike her partner, she chose to focus on her post-prison experiences:

> I did not feel like getting too stuck back there … I'm no longer an FP-25 militant. I mean … I understand that side exists within me, but I'm

> something else. It's not that I'm no longer a militant because I'm ashamed of being one. It's not that. I admit that it was a phase of my political activism … but I'm almost fifty-five years old. I have thirty years on top of my militancy. I've done many other things.

In the years that followed her militancy, Júlia seemed to undergo a gradual process of integrating her experiences as a militant: "So, when I look back, it's more like a cloud, not something concrete … I mean … there are many mirrors and many curtains between what I am today and what I was then". In this sense, Júlia displayed the I-position *I as a former militant who is not ashamed*, but paired it with the meta-position *I as a critic and reflective political activist*. This meta-position allowed her to come to terms with the fact that she was no longer an FP-25 militant, but, at the same time, it left her in no doubt that she understood the social and political reality of both the past and the present.

Júlia displayed another meta-position: *I as an activist who is disappointed with Marxist ideas.* This position incorporated her gradual disenchantment with core aspects of Marxism–Leninism:

> The Marxist left used to say that when the proletariat has nothing to do, it only has one thing to do, which is the revolution. They were deceived because when people have nothing to lose, they lose their minds and therefore can't build anything.

This meta-position gave particular voice to Júlia's cynicism about the transformative power of a vanguard (which some FP-25 members claimed the organisation to be) and the legitimacy of its actions:

> What was wrong and what we couldn't understand at the time was that the confrontation has to have a broad base. It has to have an actual and consolidated social aspect. It can't be a group of people who elect themselves as the solution.

This new ideological perspective seemed to be in coalition with another meta-position regarding the use of violence: *I as a former militant who is looking for more effective ways to achieve social transformation*. Júlia expressed this position when insisting that she hopes to find alternative solutions for social conflict, since the violent means employed by the FP-25 did not deliver the expected results: "It's not enough to kill employers … It takes much more than that. To tell you the truth, we haven't found the way to solve it yet, but I haven't given up".

Despite the dominance of these counter-violence I-positions, Júlia was clearly still aware of injustices in the social fabric: "Frankly, this is a reading of social reality that I have maintained throughout the years, because I think that the state is run to protect those who have money. It's very simple". In this sense, Júlia, like Jaime and Mariana, displayed the I-position *I as a former militant who still thinks that violence is defensible*. It was subjugated, but she relied on it to justify the FP-25's violent actions:

> I don't regret the actions carried out by the organisation and therefore I don't distance myself from the decisions that have been made … Those who have read a bit of history know that social transformations are almost always achieved through violent confrontations.

Interestingly, the weakened voice and more flexible expression of this pro-violence position seemed to be due to the fact that it was in dialogue with the counter-violence meta-position *I as a former militant who is looking for more effective ways to achieve social transformation*. Indeed, Júlia reaffirmed her desire to keep searching for alternative means of achieving social transformation:

> I still think that the social reality is deeply unjust … and it is necessary to change it, even though I don't have the formula for doing so. But I keep trying different proposals, solutions, sometimes with more conviction, other times with less conviction.

Moreover, Júlia's I-position *I as a mother* was strongly reinforced during her time in prison: "It was the time to digest the concept in the affective sense: how could we recover from a certain sloppiness towards the kids, sloppiness in the sense of neglecting our role as parents?" This led her to decide that, "when I leave prison, I will dedicate the next ten years to my children. And that's what I did". Thus, Júlia was able to negotiate clear boundaries between her family and political I-positions, and these subsequently remained in dialogue and continued to express their respective voices in her self-system:

> I have a goal, but it is no longer the *only* goal. I wouldn't endanger my relationships with my children again in the name of a political conviction … Today, it's simple: I'm politically active, but I don't go to meetings, demonstrations, or anything else on my children's birthdays. Those are sacred days … My priorities have clearly turned around. For me, today, it's clear that personal relationships are the key to my personal well-being, and that personal well-being allows me to have good relationships with others and to give something to others. So, I've clearly reversed the logic.

Júlia's political reasoning clearly changed over time. The development of different meta-positions allowed her to develop a more coherent and comprehensive self-narrative, encompassing the multiple voices of differentiated I-positions in an integrated manner, which left her more open to and prepared for change. While she preferred not to focus on her militancy as her "medal", Jaime, by contrast, still reflected on his involvement with the political struggle in order to make sense of the person he became later in life. His militancy gave him a sense of fulfilment, of being someone who fought until the last minute, and endured all the consequences of his choices with dignity.

Conclusion

Although they had long since disengaged from their respective politically violent organisations, most of the former militants felt that their politicised identity systems had remained essentially unaltered over the years. However, their political strategies had changed and, in some cases, their socio-political views had evolved, because they could now look at the past through the prism of the present. They had attained broader and more reflective knowledge of historical processes and their own past experiences.

Disengagement processes, across the different organisations under analysis, were triggered by three main factors: achievement of collective goals; personal and/or organisational issues; and arrest. Moreover, the type of disengagement trigger and the historical moment that framed each organisation both seemed to have significant impacts on the former militants' reintegration into society. In this sense, most of the pre- and counter-revolution militants disengaged from the armed struggle when their respective organisations dissolved. They felt that their political goals had been achieved and, in most cases, they did not face prison sentences. These circumstances facilitated not only their disengagement but also their successful reintegration into society. In this context, their accounts displayed victorious I-positions, such as *I as former militant who did not quit* and *I as a militant who achieved his/her goals.*

The case of the post-revolution militants was undeniably different. A democratic regime could not forgive an armed organisation that had challenged the political establishment and targeted human lives. Thus, many of these militants' reintegration into society was both delayed and complicated by a significant prison sentence. Their incarceration also contributed to a sense of defeat that was symbolised by the collective position *We as part of an organisation which was defeated.* Moreover, this sense of failure was exacerbated by the fact that some militants accepted an amnesty while in prison. According to those who rejected this amnesty, accepting it would have equated to an apology and an acknowledgement that they had done something wrong. Thus, a few militants served their full terms, anchoring their identity systems in the I-position *I as a militant who has to pay the price for my militancy* in order to keep their dignity intact.

When reflecting on the past, most of the militants, across all of the organisations under analysis, displayed the I-positions *I as a proud former militant* and *I as someone who has retained my core values.* Through these I-positions, they affirmed the continuity and coherence of their identity systems over time. Yet, a few militants recognised that their socio-political views had evolved and changed in response to the knowledge they had gained simply by being in the present and having access to both national- and international-level history. In some cases, these changes were responsible for their ongoing disengagement from the armed struggle, which was underpinned by meta-positions such as *I as a critic and reflective political activist* and *I as a former militant who is looking for more effective ways to achieve social transformation.* These meta-positions have allowed former militants to reassess and create new meanings regarding their past militancy, as well as regarding who they are and what they do today as disengaged militants. In this sense, they felt that their militancy had a valued place in their past – *I as someone who achieved the goals of my youth* – but they have moved on and lived through a variety of other, equally important, experiences in their professional, social, and family lives. Thus, everything – past, present, and imagined future – seemed to have a place in their identity systems.

This was not the case for all of the former militants, however. Some were unsure about their past choices, which was represented in the I-position *I as a former militant who doubts the merit of my past choices.* Others were still using their past militancy as their life compass. They remained disengaged from the armed struggle not because they stopped believing in the merits of political violence, but because they lost the battle and were now too old to practise it. Accordingly, the I-position *I as a former militant who still thinks that violence is defensible* was discernible in several of the militants' political narratives. However, despite holding radicalisation-prone positions, these militants did not plan to re-engage in the armed struggle. Instead, they remained determined to do what they could to improve society, which was displayed through the I-position *I as a former militant who is still civically and politically active.*

References

Ashour, O. (2009) *The de-radicalization of jihadists: transforming armed Islamist movements.* New York: Routledge.

Horgan, J. (2009) *Walking away from terrorism: accounts of disengagement from radical and extremist movements.* London: Routledge.

Randall, W. L. (2010) 'The narrative complexity of our past: in praise of memory's sins', *Theory and Psychology*, 20(2), pp. 147–169.

Reinares, F. (2011) 'Exit from terrorism: a qualitative empirical study on disengagement and deradicalization among members of ETA', *Terrorism and Political Violence*, 23 (5), pp. 780–803.

Zulaika, J. and Douglass, W. (1996) *Terror and taboo: the follies, fables and faces of terrorism.* London: Routledge.

Conclusion

I have traced the storylines in which former politically violent militants in Portugal were moulded as subjects through their interactions with the social and political contexts of their time. Therefore, former militants' stories were the focus of this book, rather than precisely how things happened in the past. Through dialogical narrative identity lenses, I have been able to examine the political narratives shaping former militants' lives, shedding light on how such political narratives impacted their past experiences and how they have been put at the service of their present selves. My focus has been on the specific issue of political violence in Portugal, rather than political violence in general. However, this does not limit the conclusions of this book to this particular issue. On the contrary, as Clifford Geertz (1973, p. 3) has affirmed, increasing our understanding of particular cases that provide "thick descriptions" of social life can have broader implications.

In this book, I have not aimed to compare the Portuguese case with cases of political violence in other countries, interpreting similarities and differences within a theoretical framework composed of general categories. Instead, I chose to add descriptive depth and conceptual sophistication to existing accounts and understandings of political violence. In this sense, I have given prominence to the political narratives of former militants, whose stories are rarely sought or recorded, despite their strong connection to the social, cultural, political, and historical contexts that framed their engagement with and disengagement from politically violent organisations. I have also shown how people's stories of their pasts are affected by their current identity positions and how such stories play a role in people's lives, triggering decisions and behaviours. Thereby, I stand with Scott Atran (2010) in believing that studying the life stories of former politically violent activists and gaining an insight into their perspectives, experiences, and feelings facilitates the demystification of political violence as a phenomenon isolated from its time and space.

It was always my intention that the study of politically motivated violence in Portugal would generate a case study for showcasing the application of my dialogical narrative identity analytical framework. This framework makes sense of the life stories of former politically violent militants by taking into account their journeys of engagement with, life within, and disengagement from politically violent organisations. In each of these moments, I traced the identity positions displayed in former militants' political narratives, informed by the principles of the DST. In this vein, I examined processes of radicalisation and deradicalisation at the individual level, but also the macro- and meso-level contexts that, according to the former militants themselves, prompted their engagement with and encouraged their disengagement from armed organisations. By applying this analytical framework to a variety of first-hand narrative accounts, I aimed to destabilise some of the rock-hard assumptions around political violence and its actors. I hoped to create a window into the former militants' life stories to understand what led them to choose violent over non-violent political means to achieve their goals, what kept them going, and what made them stop. It is to these aims, and the ways in which the dialogical narrative identity analysis helped me achieve them, that I now turn.

Life stories and political violence

The theorisation of the life stories of former politically violent militants suggests new directions for researchers of political violence. A variety of motivations has been presented by different scholars regarding why individuals engage with and disengage from politically violent organisations. These motivations tend to be understood as push and pull factors. The application of my dialogical narrative identity analytical framework extends this research by examining how personal identity positions develop in interaction with the political narratives that inhabit individuals' spatial and temporal coordinates. My findings suggest that push and pull factors may be conceptualised as the expression of a number of positions of the self that elaborate various personal meanings involved in the processes of engagement with, life within, and disengagement from a politically violent organisation, as well as processes of radicalisation and deradicalisation. The dialogue among this multiplicity of I-positions creates meanings that influence militants' beliefs, feelings, and behaviours.

This approach to the study of political violence differs from the traditional models of mainstream terrorism studies scholars, who tend to rely on secondary data sources, producing and reproducing flat descriptions and explanations, and ignoring the voices and experiences of politically violent militants themselves. To tackle these limitations and answer the call of CTS scholars for more narrative inquiry in the study of political violence, I proposed an interdisciplinary approach, including insights from psychology, sociology, international relations, anthropology, and history.

I showed the value of moving beyond the analysis of individual, social, contextual, political, and relational factors in isolation and understanding their dynamic interplay. I suggested that exploring micro-level journeys through political violence enhances our understanding of the subject at meso- and macro-levels of analyses. This happens through detailed analysis of the way each former militant describes and organises her/his various I-positions, including the dialogues and dynamic forces that occur among them, significant others, and socio-historical positions at large. In this context, I argue that considering the micro-level accounts of former militants – specifically how they interpret and internalise the events and political narratives surrounding their political militancy – can increase our understanding of why and how politically violent organisations erupt, endure, and dissolve. It also showcases how past militancy shapes identity systems in the present, and how and why some militants change more than others. The latter seems to be particularly connected to how the organisation ends – in accordance with or against the militants' wishes – and the consequences for those militants in terms of their reintegration into society without facing criminal charges or after serving time in prison.

I am aware that focusing on the micro-level – on the life stories of former militants – means that my findings are influenced by the co-construction of meaning that occurred during the interview process. I am aware that, through their stories, the former militants represented in this book attached meanings to episodes stored in their autobiographical memories, which in itself is "an active construction embedded in a social weave of dialogues that are negotiated not only between an individual and his or her immediate social environment ... but also, equally importantly, between the individual and the larger cultural milieu" (Wang and Brockmeier, 2002, p. 47). I am aware that I have accessed certain stories on which the self relies to "adjust the past to the demands of the present and the anticipated future" (Bruner, 2003, p. 213). And I am aware that a single identity-defining episode may be told very differently in different circumstances, generating multiple life narrative storylines and constructing different identities (Mishler, 2004). Yet, how former militants tell their stories is important. How they choose to represent themselves is just as relevant – if not more so – than any (intangible) assumptions of truth or reality. They have experienced politically motivated militancy and they need to make sense of it according to the requirements of their present and imagined future. In this vein, their stories and how they are told reveal parts of their inner dialogue, showing the debates, conflicts, and negotiations that occur among numerous positions of the self to make sense of each life experience. Through this window into former militants' lives, we can gain at least some understanding of why, when, and how political violence makes sense to certain human beings.

Therefore, this book makes an important contribution to debates about political violence, in general, and political violence in Portugal, in particular. It is the first study on this subject in English, and the first to apply a dialogical narrative identity analysis informed by the DST. All previous studies have been written in Portuguese and tend to take a historiographic approach to political violence. None explores politically violent militancy's implications for the former militants' lives or what we might learn by analysing their journeys through armed organisations and their processes of radicalisation and deradicalisation. Furthermore, the former militants' accounts of their militancy reveal complex lives, identity systems, and relationships, providing an important counterbalance to the way in which they are usually depicted – as inhuman, fanatical, mad, crazed killers – in both academic and non-academic literature. Thus, by prioritising the voices of the former militants themselves, this book attempts to establish their place in the history of Portugal and in the history of political violence.

Dialogical narrative identity analysis

In addition to extending theories of political violence, my findings develop our understanding of narrative identity in the context of politically violent militancy more generally. To date, narrative identity has received little attention in the political violence literature. I argue that the study of former militants' narrative identities facilitates examination of variations in militant experiences and helps to answer some key questions, such as why individuals engage with politically violent organisations, how their commitment endures, and how it ends. Below, I explain each of these contributions in turn.

In Chapter 3, I explored former militants' lives leading up to their engagement with politically violent organisations. I traced their identity positions from their early years of life to their late teens, identified some of the core positions at the origin of their militancy, and explored how these developed. I looked at how the conflicts between opposing I-positions were resolved within the self in relation to committing part of one's life to armed struggle. I also identified specific identity positions in the complex process of radicalisation. The main lesson of this chapter is that former militants did not simply engage with politically violent organisations independently of the political narratives and experiences that populated their life stories. On the contrary, they used a variety of stories, including those of the people around them, to justify their militancy. They crafted both internal and external I-positions to give meaning to who they were in the contexts they inhabited, particularly in times of socio-political turmoil, such as during the Colonial War and in the aftermath of the April Revolution.

Thus, different life stories, populated by different contexts and relationships, gave rise to different interpretations and courses of action. For instance, for pre-revolution militants, the Colonial War was "the drop of acid that stings the eyes, causing them to open and see", as Rui from the ARA explained. Most of these militants were raised in a more or less explicitly anti-regime environment, populated by oppositional political narratives and relatives with a history of resistance. Therefore, being sent to fight in the Colonial War or fleeing into exile to avoid it created radicalisation-prone positions (e.g., *I as someone who hates the Colonial War*), which in turn encouraged engagement-prone positions (e.g., *I as someone who will make war on war*).

Counter-revolution militants had a totally different experience, even though they were from the same generation as the pre-revolution militants. Their education was marked by pro-regime narratives, strengthened by a dominant *I as a Catholic* position. In this vein, they saw the Colonial War through the regime's eyes. It was a "defence mission", as Afonso from the ELP affirmed. Thus, counter-revolution militants assimilated the external positions *My country is fighting for its people* and *My country's enemies are the communist liberation movements*, embodying the I-position *I as a soldier*. For these militants, the April Revolution, and especially the decolonisation process it triggered, came as a surprise. The former was seen as unnecessary and illegitimate, while the latter was seen as a crime that claimed numerous lives. Furthermore, counter-revolution militants feared an imminent communist takeover of Portugal due to the active role played by the PCP in the post-revolution period. Consequently, engagement-prone positions started to erupt, such as *I as a young individual who should defend my country from communism*. For these militants, armed action was justified by the need to restore order and stop left-wing expansion in Portugal on behalf of a Catholic country (*My country and its people as Catholic*) which was not communist (*My country and its people as anti-communist*).

Nevertheless, despite the centripetal movement of I-positions towards commitment to politically violent organisations, some militants recognised conflict between opposing I-positions. In the case of Henrique from the LUAR, for instance, there was a conflict between the voice of his family, enacted by the counter-engagement position *I as a father*, and the voice of fighting for freedom, represented by the pro-engagement position *I as someone who believes that risking my life is the only way of fighting the regime*. To resolve this conflict, Henrique's dialogical self developed a meta-position: *I as someone who is fighting for everybody's children*. This allowed him to live with himself as an absent father because he viewed himself as a committed militant who was fighting for the greater good. Through this meta-position, he negotiated the demands of becoming a committed militant who would fight for freedom for everyone, including his own children. This helped him to reduce the tension between two conflicting I-positions and to update his identity system from *I as a father* to *I as a committed militant*.

In Chapter 4, I demonstrated how the dynamics of life within a politically violent organisation shaped individuals' identity systems. I started by looking at one of the most identity-challenging moments in the life of any politically violent militant – going underground. This meant assuming a clandestine identity, severing contact with loved ones, giving up valued activities, and becoming a full-time militant. Thus, I again focused on how former militants attempted to resolve the conflict between opposing I-positions: those pulling them back to non-militancy (e.g., *I as a student* or *I as a mother/father*) and those pushing them into more committed militancy (e.g., *I as someone who believes that armed action is needed to assist the overthrow of the dictatorship*). In this context, it was possible to grasp the personal responsibility and sense of duty that various militants felt in politically troubled contexts to lay down their lives for a cause, especially because, in their view, very few individuals were willing to do the same, which strengthened their resolve even further. Therefore, for most militants, the challenges of life underground were mitigated by the action of the core position *I as a committed militant*. Through this core position, valued non-militancy positions were subjugated and the militant identity predominated. Moreover, this core position was apparently supported by what della Porta (2013) has termed "cognitive closure" and "affective closure". On the one hand, cognitive closure relates to militants' need to make sense of their behaviour. Across different periods of time and organisations, various militants reflected that their perceptions of the world and of their own behaviour developed in a very constrained setting. Over time, these perceptions became ever more segregated from mainstream society, impacting the militants' narratives and the value systems they adopted. This process was also influenced by the fact that the militants could not simply return to their previous lives without facing consequences, which caused them to invest more deeply in their revolutionary identities. On the other hand, affective closure forges deep and intense relationships among the members of small, closed, restricted, and restrictive organisations. For most militants, the bonds of trust created by risking their lives in armed missions fashioned a sense of shared experience. This not only helped to dampen interpersonal conflict, but also fuelled pro-commitment positions (e.g., *I as a loyal comrade*), while subjugating pro-disengagement positions (e.g., *My organisation is inefficient and unprepared*) that had the potential to destabilise the core position *I as a committed militant*.

I equally examined the gender dynamics within politically violent organisations. In most cases, women's (lack of) participation in armed actions mirrored the macro-cultural narrative *Women as housewives*. Thus, women played little or no role in some organisations and the traditional roles of wife and mother in others. They rarely participated on an equal footing to the men. Indeed, at times, male militants' views on women who played a more active role displayed the fine line between female emancipation through participation in the armed struggle and female subjugation through serving men's purposes in the armed struggle. Women were also clearly sexualised within some organisations: they were seen as militants who could use seduction to further the organisation's cause or courted as romantic partners by their male comrades.

Finally, I demonstrated why and how different armed organisations perpetrated different types of violence, and, particularly, how the former militants interpreted and justified this violence. Pre-revolution militants tended to view politically motivated violence as their final option to weaken the regime. By attacking the structures of the regime, these militants hoped to raise awareness among the Portuguese people that it was possible to resist. They were strongly against targeting human lives, rooting their identities in the I-position *I as part of a non-terrorist organisation that does not kill people*.

Counter-revolution militants justified their politically motivated violence as necessary to prevent the establishment of a communist dictatorship in

Portugal. However, they were reluctant to discuss the violent acts committed by their respective organisations. Instead, they preferred to focus on their overall objectives and the violence they could have perpetrated, but chose not to, because, particularly within the ELP, they held the position *I as part of a Catholic organisation that does not commit gratuitous violence.*

Post-revolution militants justified their politically motivated violence on the basis that it challenged the routine abuse of workers by employers and the state. In this vein, they openly targeted human lives as a political strategy, particularly "the symbols of the employers", as Júlia explained. They hoped that their actions would trigger a revolt among the workers, who would then help the FP-25 to realise the socialist promises of the April Revolution. However, the escalation of violence merely aroused fear among those who would supposedly benefit from the campaign. Later, this led some post-revolution militants to question the Marxist–Leninist ideological assumptions of a vanguard orchestrating an armed struggle, opening the way to pro-deradicalisation positions.

In Chapter 5, I explored former militants' disengagement from politically violent organisations. This tended to vary according to three distinct factors: achievement of collective goals; personal and/or organisational issues; and arrest. I also looked closely at how former militants reintegrated back into mainstream society and concluded that this process was strongly influenced by both the disengagement trigger and the historical moment that framed each organisation. In most cases, the disengagement of both pre- and counter-revolution militants was triggered by the dissolution of their organisations at a time when they were unlikely to face criminal charges (after the 1974 revolution and after the 1975 counter-revolution, respectively). Hence, the vast majority of these militants experienced relatively smooth reintegration into society. By contrast, many of the post-revolution militants were forced to disengage because they were arrested, so they had a much harder time coming to terms with the identity change from *I as a committed militant* to *I as a former militant*. In this vein, both pre- and counter-revolution militants tended to see themselves in terms of the I-position *I as a militant who achieved her/his goals*, while post-revolution militants internalised a sense of failure: *We as part of an organisation that was defeated.*

I also examined how former militants integrated their past militancy within their present selves. Most of them considered that their politicised identity systems have remained essentially unaltered over the years. This was represented by the I-positions *I as a proud former militant* and *I as someone who has retained my core values*. However, their political strategies have changed and, in some cases, their socio-political views have evolved because they can now look at the past from the perspective of the present. Consequently, they have attained broader and more reflective knowledge of historical processes and past experiences. This was made possible through the development of meta-positions, which not only stabilised the conflict among past, present, and imagined future positions, but also created new meanings, giving sense to the

I-position *I as a former militant*. Some militants certainly changed less than others, maintaining pro-radicalisation positions over the decades, including *I as a former militant who still thinks that violence is defensible*. However, dominant (or at least equivalent) pro-disengagement positions, such as *I as a mother/father*, had kept them away from the armed struggle in recent years.

In summary, throughout Chapters 3, 4, and 5, I explored not only the meaning-making processes underpinning the human need to give sense to life experiences, but also how the multivocal self dialogically manages the demands of several I-positions. I showed that times of socio-political turmoil led individuals to challenge the prevailing political narratives according to the identity positions that took root in their selves in the early years of their lives. I displayed how anchoring the identity system in certain core positions enabled the management of several micro-dialogues in the vocal society that is the self. These core positions helped to mitigate conflict and kept the tension between opposing I-positions at a bearable level. Finally, I demonstrated the importance of meta-positions as conflict mediators. These meta-positions underpinned certain militants' engagement decisions but also supported ongoing disengagement. In short, they have allowed former militants to integrate who they were, who they are, and who they will become.

References

Atran, S. (2010) *Talking to the enemy: violent extremism, sacred values and what it means to be human*. London: Penguin Books.

Bruner, J. (2003) 'Self-making narratives', in Fivush, R. and Haden, C. A. (eds) *Autobiographical memory and the construction of a narrative self*. Mahwah, NJ: Erlbaum, pp. 209–226.

della Porta, D. (2013) *Clandestine political violence*. Cambridge: Cambridge University Press.

Geertz, C. (1973) *The interpretation of cultures*. New York: Basic Books.

Mishler, E. (2004) 'Historians of the self: restoring lives, revising identities', *Research in Human Development*, 1(1), pp. 101–121.

Wang, Q. and Brockmeier, J. (2002) 'Autobiographical remembering as cultural practice: understanding the interplay between memory, self and culture', *Culture and Psychology*, 8(1), pp. 45–64.

Index

Please note that references to Notes are indicated by the letter 'n' followed by the Note number. Page references to Tables are in *italics*.